PRINCIPAL
LABS

Megan Kortlandt   Carly Stone   Samantha Keesling

PRINCIPAL LABS

Strengthening
Instructional Leadership
Through Shared Learning

ascd

Alexandria, Virginia USA

1703 N. Beauregard St. • Alexandria, VA 22311-1714 USA
Phone: 800-933-2723 or 703-578-9600 • Fax: 703-575-5400
Website: www.ascd.org • Email: member@ascd.org
Author guidelines: www.ascd.org/write

Ranjit Sidhu, *CEO & Executive Director;* Penny Reinart, *Chief Impact Officer;* Genny Ostertag, *Senior Director, Acquisitions & Editing;* Susan Hills, *Senior Acquisitions Editor;* Julie Houtz, *Director, Book Editing;* Megan Doyle, *Editor;* Thomas Lytle, *Creative Director;* Donald Ely, *Art Director;* Samantha Wood, *Graphic Designer;* Melissa Johnston, *Graphic Designer;* Keith Demmons, *Senior Production Designer;* Kelly Marshall, *Production Manager;* Shajuan Martin, *E-Publishing Specialist*

All web links in this book are correct as of the publication date below but may have become inactive or otherwise modified since that time. If you notice a deactivated or changed link, please email books@ascd.org with the words "Link Update" in the subject line. In your message, please specify the web link, the book title, and the page number on which the link appears.

PAPERBACK ISBN: 978-1-4166-3044-9   ASCD product #122005   n8/21
PDF E-BOOK ISBN: 978-1-4166-3045-6; see Books in Print for other formats.
Quantity discounts are available: email programteam@ascd.org or call 800-933-2723, ext. 5773, or 703-575-5773. For desk copies, go to www.ascd.org/deskcopy.

Library of Congress Cataloging-in-Publication Data
Names: Kortlandt, Megan, author. | Stone, Carly, author. | Keesling, Samantha, author.
Title: Principal labs : strengthening instructional leadership through shared learning / Megan Kortlandt, Carly Stone, Samantha Keesling.
Description: Alexandria, Virginia : ASCD, 2021. | Includes bibliographical references.
Identifiers: LCCN 2021017500 (print) | LCCN 2021017501 (ebook) | ISBN 9781416630449 (paperback) | ISBN 9781416630456 (pdf)
Subjects: LCSH: Principals—Training of. | Professional learning communities. | Laboratory schools.
Classification: LCC LB2831.9 .K67 2021 (print) | LCC LB2831.9 (ebook) | DDC 371.2/012—dc23
LC record available at https://lccn.loc.gov/2021017500
LC ebook record available at https://lccn.loc.gov/2021017501

30 29 28 27 26 25 24 23 22 21   1 2 3 4 5 6 7 8 9 10 11 12

PRINCIPAL LABS

1. Principal Labs: What They Are and Why They Matter —————— 1

2. Planning and Structuring a Lab ———————————— 8

3. Laying the Groundwork ——————————————— 27

4. Labs to Introduce New Curriculum ————————— 45

5. Labs to Study Instructional Practices ————————— 65

6. Labs to Build a Network of Leaders ————————— 87

7. Labs to Foster Collaborative Aspirations ———————— 105

8. Logistics —————————————————————— 118

Acknowledgments ————————————————— 134

Appendix: The Clipboard ———————————————— 136

References ——————————————————————— 146

Index ————————————————————————— 149

About the Authors ————————————————— 155

1

Principal Labs: What They Are and Why They Matter

Lately, there has been an awful lot of research confirming what so many of us probably already know: that building leaders have a tremendous impact on the success of the students in their schools. As evaluators, mentors, and an everyday presence in the school, building leaders are the most influential sources of feedback for teachers, so they must take on the role of lead learners themselves. Although we may recognize the importance of administrators as instructional leaders, developing their capacity to do so is something that doesn't get nearly as much attention as it deserves. Between busy schedules and limited budgets, professional learning for principals often takes a backseat to the many other obligations of their jobs. Moreover, when instructional leaders are fortunate enough to be able to prioritize their own learning, the options are slim.

Principals can and do choose to attend administrative conferences, but the focus is often outside the scope of classroom instruction. While there may be a few choices focused on developing instructional leadership, the bulk of the offerings centers around scheduling, board relations, and athletics—in short, all of the things that keep administrators' attention away from where its impact is greatest: the classroom. Even when a session might address the needs of an instructional leader, the nature of these conferences often feels like it's a one-and-done experience, so ongoing support for this work is hard to come by.

Resources like emails, webinars, and podcasts arrive in administrators' already stacked inboxes. Although these resources can keep leaders up to date, they can also have the unintended consequence of further isolating those who are already, in many cases, feeling very much on their own in their professional learning journey.

Similarly, over the past few years as research on coaching effectiveness has grown, administrators have begun the practice of hiring their own coaches. While this is a much-needed support and can indeed assist principals in goal setting, reflection, and transfer of learning, it is largely still independent learning.

In order to truly take on the work of becoming lead learners, building leaders must engage in professional collaboration. Fullan and Quinn (2016) explain, "If one wants to shift school, district, or system practices, one needs to have a strong learning design *and* deeper collaborative work" (p. 62). Any administrator who has ever been lucky enough to work with a strong, collaborative team would quickly recognize this. But between the daily demands of a busy building and increasingly limited resources, there is a significant gap between the demand for collaborative professional learning focused on instructional leadership and the everyday implementation of it.

A Growing Need for Support

It's no secret that recent years in education have seen a tremendous rise in pressure. Between the adoption of increasingly rigorous standards to a rapidly changing landscape of legislation and evaluation, stakes are high. And it's showing. A 2019 report from the Economic Policy Institute states that the shortage of credentialed teachers, especially in areas of high poverty, "is real, large and growing, and worse than we thought" (Garcia & Weiss, 2019). What's more is that, while the media may focus on the shortage of teachers, the same is true for building leaders. In their book *Design Thinking for School Leaders: Five Roles and Mindsets That Ignite Positive Change*, Gallagher and Thordarson (2018) cite research that shows an annual principal turnover rate of 20 percent overall among public school principals and 30 percent in schools that may be considered "troubled."

While it may be tempting to blame teacher and principal turnover on factors like compensation, it's not that simple. Support, or lack thereof, is equally—if not more—prevalent. The same 2019 report from the Economic Policy Institute on teacher shortages cites lack of training and support as one of the major factors driving teachers from the profession. For a workforce that is increasingly comprised of millennials, research is emerging on what is needed to retain this growing demographic. Liana Loewus (2018) explains that central to their values are aspirations of leadership and needs for ongoing support and feedback. The need to support principals so that they, in turn, feel confident and well-equipped to give this necessary feedback is more important than ever.

Likewise, the National Association of Secondary School Principals (NASSP) and National Association of Elementary School Principals (NAESP) (2013) found that primary reasons principals leave their jobs include feeling isolated and unprepared. As it turns out, principals aren't feeling too different from teachers in their need for support and collaboration.

Support That Sticks

Learning Forward's standards for professional learning emphasize the need for feedback and reflection as well as for learning to occur within the context of collaborative teams:

> Learning communities convene regularly and frequently during the workday to engage in collaborative professional learning to strengthen their practice and increase student results. Learning community members are accountable to one another to achieve the shared goals of the school and school system and work in transparent, authentic settings that support their improvement. (Learning Forward, 2021)

Building this collaborative culture sounds far simpler than it is, and the bulk of the responsibility often falls to principals who are already overloaded.

Because this is such a complex and nuanced process, the professional learning that principals themselves are participating in should model the same collaborative culture. So, while the content of the professional learning for principals must be grounded in research, so, too, must the practices. Professional learning that will truly support instructional leaders—and through them, their teachers—must

- Be collaborative.
- Include modeling.
- Be job embedded.
- Allow for reflection.
- Offer opportunities for coaching and transfer.

Where Principal Labs Come In

Although huge strides have been made to structure professional learning for teachers in this way, it is long overdue that we take this research about professional learning to create structures that support instructional leaders. Any professional learning that is going to truly meet the needs of developing instructional leaders should address three major goals:

1. **Build relationships among all stakeholders.** The research is clear on the power of professional collaboration and collective efficacy. And with so many people—from superintendents to building principals to instructional coaches—invested in instruction and supporting the cognitive and noncognitive aspects of student growth, it's important to intentionally cultivate collaborative partnerships in order to carry the learning beyond each experience.

2. **Calibrate thinking about students' and teachers' needs.** This will help principals to be able to strategically offer feedback for teachers that is aligned, relevant, and responsive.

3. **Capitalize on time spent in professional learning.** Because of the many demands and responsibilities of a building leader, it's crucial to both minimize the amount of time spent away from principals' buildings and to maximize the time spent with relevant experience and actionable discoveries. To us, this means that we need to keep the learning as close to the context of principals' buildings as possible through job-embedded professional learning opportunities.

Anyone who has ever designed or planned any professional learning surely recognizes that these three goals, though they may sound simple, are anything but. With seemingly infinite idiosyncrasies that are a natural by-product of the human nature of our work, calibrating feedback can be a surprisingly complex process. And, as just about anyone who

has ever struggled to navigate workplace dynamics knows, building relationships is no easy feat. Neither of these goals can (or should) be done
in isolation—or in isolation of the primary focus to build instructional
leadership that is responsive to teachers' and students' needs. This is
where principal labs come in.

The principal lab is a structure that we developed as a part of one
district's professional learning system when we recognized this complex
need for support. These labs designed specifically for building and district administrators are tailored to their needs as instructional leaders.
While structures like instructional rounds work to scratch the surface,
principal labs offer a deep, intentional dive into supporting the whole
instructional system—with leaders as the primary focus. Principal labs
offer a structure for scalable, flexible job-embedded professional learning that combines instructional rounds and peer coaching in the context
of a collaborative network of support. Within this structure of principal
labs, which we'll detail in Chapter 2, principals build relationships with
their colleagues to collaborate and form a network of professional learning, participate in an anchoring experience to work toward a common
understanding or language of the lab's focus, and engage in at least one
observation where they see the focus of the day's lab in action in their
own buildings. Principal labs move deeper beyond instructional rounds
by tying these observations to their anchoring experience and then
through the facilitated reflection that happens after the observations.
This component of the lab implements tenets of coaching to help principals reflect and analyze what they've experienced and make decisions
about next steps forward.

We initially designed the labs when we recognized a principal-shaped
hole in our support system, and we found that, when we combined principal labs with other structures like PLCs, school improvement plans,
and teacher learning labs, this administrator-centered professional
learning can impact positive change in the whole school, district, and
educational community.

The Lab's Impact

When working together in a district of approximately 10,000 students
and more than 25 administrators, we knew we had to be systematic
about the *who gets what and when* of professional learning. To do this, we

synthesized research related to student learning and applied it to adult learning.

It was already established as a part of the district's culture that administrators attend professional learning alongside their teachers, and the practice of engaging in instructional rounds had been in place for a number of years. Still, though, something was missing. We assumed that having administrators participate in professional learning alongside their teachers would be enough, but it wasn't. There was tremendous benefit in their participation, but it was easy for a principal to spend a lot of time attending to initiatives for many different content areas and grade levels, and they sometimes reported they got lost in teacher learning and didn't know how to prioritize this time or effectively support teachers.

Principal labs offer the opportunity to ensure that administrators more deeply understand the instructional initiatives in their buildings and can more confidently support the work teachers are doing. Once we introduced principal labs, we quickly started to see gains. Instructional practices began to shift in meaningful and consistent ways to create a shared understanding of how best practices play out in the district's classrooms. And, what's more, collaborative networks really started to gel in authentic ways. Principals began to feel more comfortable reaching out to one another and to those in the central office as collaborators, and teachers started to report that feedback from their administrators was more aligned with the professional learning and risk taking they'd been doing.

In education, it often seems like anything you try to initiate is just a drop in the bucket—unlikely to have any lasting effect in a field where it feels like everything is working against us. It's true that without an intentional, systemic plan for support and without a coherent, collaborative team, any sort of instructional change will struggle to gain traction. But, with principal labs, we've found a means for systemic support and a deepened culture for professional learning that maximizes principals' time and builds efficacy for all involved. With an understanding of the beliefs, structure, variations, and logistics required, we believe that any member of the team—from consultants, coaches, and central office to building principals themselves—can plan and facilitate effective principal labs. No matter where you may fall in this range of roles, we hope this book will help you do that.

In the first three chapters of this book, we'll share with you our beliefs and the research that make up the foundation of principal labs, and we'll describe some tools to put those beliefs and research into action. The goal is not that you execute a cookie-cutter template, but that you can use the elements of the principal lab structure to design professional learning that is responsive to the needs of any group you work with. Chapters 4–7 will bring theory to action with real-world examples from different types of impactful labs we've run. And, in Chapter 8, we'll share logistics that can help make planning your own principal lab a success.

By reading this book, we hope you'll gain an understanding of the value of principal labs, research-based common elements that yield a successful lab experience for all, and tips and tricks to try along the way. We are thrilled to share with you a practice that has been the single most effective move we've made to transform leading and learning through shared learning, and we hope you'll walk away with the tools you need to make principal labs your own.

2

Planning and Structuring a Lab

Principal labs are a form of job-embedded professional learning, which means that they occur during the school day in the context of the principals' everyday lives. They borrow from the well-known and highly impactful structures for professional learning of instructional labs, instructional rounds, and peer coaching.

Outside the realm of professional learning, the term "lab" often has the connotation of putting hypotheses into action. This is true for principal labs as well. In a principal lab, participants will

- Engage in new learning. This may take the form of research and/or modeling around instructional needs or initiatives.
- Observe classroom instruction to analyze how the learning looks "in action."
- Plan together for support and feedback through collaborative coaching.

Together, the three of us have facilitated dozens and dozens of principal labs for elementary, middle, and high school principals. Our labs have ranged from studying early literacy to algebra instruction, from collaboration to social emotional learning. Through these varied experiences, we've found that no two labs are exactly the same. As a hallmark of job-embedded professional learning, we strive to make principal labs responsive to what participants need in their context at that moment, so prior to each lab, we are gathering formal and informal data, listening to participants, and planning for facilitation that will be the best fit for the day. Although the details of our facilitation shifted with each lab, we found that they all took on a similar shape and structure when it came to who was involved and how the day was mapped out.

Who's in the Room

Although we've given them the colloquial name of "principal labs," attendance is not—should not—be limited to principals. Indeed, principals are the key players. But, for principal labs, it's important to gather stakeholders across the instructional leadership structure to support the principals in their learning. That means including curriculum directors, assistant superintendents, curriculum consultants, and instructional coaches to form a united team. In their article studying the research on "Leadership Content Knowledge," Stein and Nelson (2003) explain the need for having a vertical alignment of many roles in the room:

> Professional development for teachers is not sufficient to change instructional practice, especially across an entire system. Teachers must believe that serious engagement in their own learning is part and parcel of what it means to be a professional and they must expect to be held accountable for continuously improving instructional practice. Similarly, principals must not only be capable of providing professional development for their teachers, but also have the knowledge, skills, and strength of character to hold teachers accountable for integrating what they have learned in professional development into their ongoing practice. District leaders, in turn, must be able to support principals' learning and be knowledgeable enough to be able to hold principals accountable in a fair way. Given their roles as both supporters and evaluators, administrators constitute a critical leverage point in the systemic improvement of instruction. (p. 425)

We know, as Stein and Nelson confirm, that student cognitive and non-cognitive growth doesn't happen in isolation; it is part of a larger, supportive system. Acknowledging this and recognizing that it applies to building leaders as well means that instructional leaders in many roles and capacities should not only be invited to the principal labs—they should make it a priority. While it might not be realistic (or beneficial) to have everyone from every role in the room for every lab, thinking strategically about having a vertical alignment in the room will ensure that all of the participants are systemically supported.

While we've found that it's beneficial to have that vertical alignment of roles in the room in terms of principals and those in the central office who support them, we've also learned that you sometimes need to think about the scope and audience of the principals you want to involve. For example, when we recognized a need for shared learning about guided reading in elementary buildings, we invited elementary principals but not principals from the district's secondary buildings. When we had a lesson with a broader focus, like lesson design and the gradual release of responsibility, we found that it yielded richer discussion and deeper thinking when K–12 colleagues were together for the lab. In both cases, central office administrators were still invited to achieve that vertical alignment in learning, but we were purposeful in inviting a focused group of the principals for whom the lab was designed to support.

The Structure of a Principal Lab

Although the purpose and the order of the agenda for each lab experience may vary, there are a few essential elements to implementing a principal lab. For each full-day lab, we designed opportunities for relationship building, an anchoring experience, shared observation, as well as feedback and feeding forward. How we ordered these and tailored them to fit the needs of that particular day's learning varied widely, but we found that keeping these four basic elements at the heart of the structure helped us design learning that was meaningful and lasting for all of the participants. See Figure 2.1 for an overview of these four elements that we will detail throughout this chapter.

Relationship Building

As previously mentioned, principal labs are composed of a wide range of instructional leadership stakeholders, and we use the term "stakeholders" intentionally; everyone sitting around the table should have a deep commitment to the work being done from within their varying roles. Having this range of roles at the table presents a unique set of challenges. You might be bringing together people who have vied for promotions or positions against each other, or who come from rival schools.

FIGURE 2.1

Essential Elements

Essential Elements	Suggested Components
Relationship building	• Icebreakers • Team-building activities • Reflective activities • Points of pride • Intentional grouping
Anchoring experience	• Demonstration lesson • Anchor article
Shared observation	• Whole lesson • Learning looks
Feedback and feeding forward	• Personal reflection • Observation analysis • Data dig • Collaborative coaching • Responsive planning • Commitment making

Bringing in administrators from the central office also means that the people who do the principals' evaluations are in the room alongside the principals, which can affect the dynamic significantly. Much like Viviane Robinson (2011) explains that principals should learn alongside their teachers, though, we have found that it's just as important for central office teaching and learning leadership to learn alongside their principals. Just as principals may have varying backgrounds, so, too, do central office administrators, and these labs provide an opportunity to deepen and broaden everyone's experience and understanding of what it means to support instruction in their district. What's more, principal labs involve examining instructional practices, vulnerabilities, and our own growth. This is deeply emotional work that speaks to educators' hearts and their profession, so we know that this is not something that will be accomplished with a simple committee meeting. Because it is an ongoing, adaptive process of learning, principal labs strive to form truly collaborative partnerships among all of the participants.

When you're dealing with attendees who have busy schedules, it would be easy to want to cut right to the chase of the learning so as to not waste any valuable time. But don't underestimate the importance of carving out some of that time during each lab to purposefully work on building relationships. This could mean starting with some icebreaker-style games and working your way up to cooperative, team-building activities to help your participants better understand their leadership styles and how they can work together. Depending on the comfort level and relationships of the team, we choose among three activity categories that push participants to different levels of intimacy and vulnerability:

- **Icebreakers** are basic connecting activities meant to get participants talking, laughing, and connecting. These are usually pretty low risk and could include super basic sentence starters to get to know each other, like two truths and a lie or "stand up if you. . . ." You might choose an icebreaker if you are just starting your lab experiences and your participants don't know one another very well yet.

- **Team-building activities** are a step further than icebreakers, as they require members to work together toward a common goal. Breakout rooms and challenges that require all members of the team to contribute toward solving a problem can be especially helpful here. You might choose this type of connector if you're looking to build or strengthen the way your team members connect with one another.

- **Reflective activities** support people in understanding one another's experiences, beliefs, and personalities more intimately. A reflective activity might ask participants to answer questions about their leadership or learning styles to determine which color, animal, or category they fit into so that they can better identify characteristics and strengths that they hold within these varying styles. They might also ask principals to reflect on the lab's topic in relation to their own experiences with a question like "What did a typical math lesson look like when you were in high school?" These reflective activities can be the most powerful experiences for relationship building. Oftentimes these experiences require participants to look forward, backward, or inward to reflect on how their beliefs and their experiences may impact their leadership.

Games and trust exercises alone are not enough, though, so throughout the labs, it's important to be purposeful in establishing groupings to make sure that stakeholders from varying experiences and positions share the conversation together. Just as teachers are thoughtful to grouping students according to their strengths, partner your collaborative teams according to their strengths and roles.

It's also important in building relationships to take into consideration how you structure your discussions. It's easy to fall into the trap of assuming that, since everyone in the room is a professional, they all have the same readiness to engage in collaborative discussions. Intentionally structuring not only who works together, but also how they engage in those discussions, can help participants to build entry points into discussions and growing collegial relationships with each other. We want to be intentional about not having too many people with a similar role in the same group, spreading out new members of the administration team across groups, and breaking apart folks who already worked together in buildings so that we can create diverse opportunities for rich discussion and experiences. For nearly every lab we've facilitated, we've grouped participants in slightly different ways. In a lab that brought together principals across all grade levels K–12, we grouped participants into principals of schools that fed into each other. In another, which we'll detail further in Chapter 7, principals formed groups based on an area of inquiry they were studying in their buildings. In another lab, we extended our connector activity, in which principals took a quiz to determine their leadership style and grouped them so that they had members of their group from varying leadership styles. Sometimes our groupings stemmed from previous conversations and learning we'd had with them. For example, if we knew that some principals were taking on a leading edge in the day's focus, we flowed between having them work with each other and spreading them out between several groups. In the chapters that follow, we'll explore in detail some of the different ways you may consider structuring discussions to further build these relationships.

One agenda item that can help your team to build relationships—especially if you're planning for principal labs with participants across multiple buildings—is to highlight **points of pride.** As busy as administrators are, they rarely get the opportunity to really get to know buildings other than their own, which can contribute to feeling like a district of many separate schools rather than one cohesive school district. It is important not to underestimate the necessity of this work.

The premise for celebrating points of pride is fairly simple: you ask principals to engage in a kind of grown-up show-and-tell. In one of our early series of principal labs, each time participants met, the team rotated to a different building. For each lab, the first 30 minutes on the agenda were set aside for a principal from the host building to take participants on a small tour or to show off some of their particular points of pride from their buildings and classrooms. This helped establish the host buildings as having a lot to celebrate and give, which was crucial groundwork in a lab setting that can run the risk of feeling critical, and it helped every stakeholder feel pride in buildings that were not their own.

In a later series, each time the participants met, they brought one point of pride to verbally share with the whole group at the opening of the lab. Points of pride ranged from a high school principal sharing the good news that a student athlete had signed with a major university, to an elementary principal sharing that an intervention initiative was showing strong results.

Anchoring Experience

For each lab, the facilitating team should plan for a piece of shared learning to ground and extend the group's discussions. One of the hallmarks of effective professional learning is that it includes "models and modeling of effective practice" (Darling-Hammond, Hyler, & Gardner, 2017). In some cases, a curriculum consultant or district teacher might engage participants in a sample lesson from a particular content area, and in other cases, you might work with a reading protocol to study an academic article related to the day's focus.

Demonstration Lesson. Before going into in-practice classrooms, you want to give participants a strong foundation to help them understand what they will be studying. You may engage them as learners in a model lesson. For example, in an elementary lab where administrators were studying math models, the principals engaged in a lesson that asked them to make sense of multiplication using different mathematical representations. They experienced this through the student lens to better understand what the experience was like as a learner. The district's math consultant then helped them unpack what she'd done instructionally to help them make the necessary connections between their mathematical representation and deepen their understanding of multiplication. This helped principals understand why multiple representations are important and how teachers productively engage students in making sense of and connecting representations. To facilitate a demonstration lesson like this, you may invite a teacher with expertise in the area to join you for this part of the lab, or you may employ a curriculum consultant. This may also be a good time to reach out to your ISD or consultants with your curriculum publisher. If a live lesson isn't doable, you can use a video of a lesson, too. Because lab time is often very tightly packed, a demonstration lesson should be fairly quick—no more than 30 minutes (not including the debrief). No matter how or who you get to facilitate this, a demonstration lesson should provide the principals the opportunity to experience the lab's focus as a learner and then unpack the moves they experienced.

Anchor Article. If you don't think that participants could observe what they need from a model lesson in that limited time frame, you may need to look toward other sources. In this case, we use the term "article" broadly. Although we most frequently use a shared article, you may find that you anchor principals in any of the following:

- One short, shared text
- A choice of multiple texts or excerpts
- Artifacts from curriculum
- Teacher-submitted lesson plans
- Examples of student work

If your lab calls for a need to anchor your learning in research or if you are making a shift and you want to take any potential for personal bias out of it, using an anchor article to ground the group's understanding can be helpful, as it brings other voices and research into the room. For example, in a lab studying student engagement, we read together Strong, Silver, and Robinson's (1995) article "Strengthening Student Engagement." As principals read this article, we engaged them in a structured protocol for annotating and discussing to determine the engagement criteria they'd inquire about throughout the remainder of the lab. Having this common text helped put everyone on the same playing field with common language to use as they continued the learning together.

Likewise, you may want to anchor your participants in texts or artifacts that broaden their own experiences and reflections, but an outside article may be too removed. In this case, you may use samples of student work or teacher-submitted lesson plans to anchor your participants in the day's focus. In one lab to study writing instruction in 3rd grade classrooms, principals brought student samples that they felt represented a range of student skills. They connected with a colleague from another building to collaboratively analyze the samples and recognize common-alities across the district. Later in the lab, then, principals could return to their analysis to develop questions and inferences that tied to what they saw and learned throughout the day.

Each anchoring experience should come from ongoing feedback and conversations with building principals and should be directly tied to the purpose of that day's lab. If, for example, several administrators report that their math teachers are struggling with their new curriculum, your lab and its anchoring experience should focus on this. Participants may experience a lesson from the new curriculum from the students' per-spective, or they may review some research that grounded the district's decision in adopting the new resource. Having a shared experience will help your team gain some common language and understanding, but more important, it frames everyone as learners—a crucial element of principal labs that is key to establishing a trusting team dynamic. Whether a shared reading or lesson, the anchoring experience will estab-lish a lens for the day's observations and discussions.

Shared Observation

Much like a teacher lab experience, at the core of the principal lab is the shared observation. During this time, participants go into the classroom of a teacher or teachers who are actively taking on work related to the learning focus of the lab. We call these teachers our **hosts**. Through these opportunities to see learning in action, participants can gain a better ref-erence point to where teachers are working within a learning continuum.

Choosing host classrooms for participants to visit can be a nuanced part of planning a lab. Depending on the purpose of a lab, you may want to choose host teachers who are at the forefront of the school's learning edge, or you may want to choose teachers who represent how instruc-tion in most classrooms looks. You might expect to encounter a wide variety of responses and anxieties in asking a teacher to bring a group of administrators into their classroom to watch them teach, too. As a whole we found that, once we explained that the principal lab participants are coming in as learners for the purpose of deepening their understanding of the teachers' work so they can be more supportive, teachers were enthusiastic about the project. Still, navigating the vulnerabilities and emotions of hosts is something that requires thoughtful planning and attention to emotional intelligence. In the chapters that follow, we'll detail more about how we chose hosts for particular types of labs and purposes, and we'll explain how we ensured that the hosts were prepared and supported for the experience.

Depending on the purpose of the day's lab, your shared observation might take on a variety of different overall structures.

Whole Lesson. For these, participants watch an entire lesson or class period from beginning to end, but you may choose how you divide your participants. We found that, when norming was important to the purpose of the lab, we wanted all participants to observe the same class, so we all went into the same class to observe the same lesson at the same time. This was a helpful experience for us when we were studying a new approach to teaching grammar in context. It was important to us that all principals at the lab had consistency in their observation experience so that they could calibrate together on the instructional moves that they saw, so we all traveled to observe the same lesson. Sometimes, though, we wanted to cast a wider net to bring more than one experience back to deepen the discussions, so we split participants into smaller groups to visit multiple classrooms in parallel observations. In Chapter 4, you'll read about a lab we facilitated to study new curriculum where we split into smaller groups to visit several algebra classes so that we could cast a wider net in our observation experiences. In some cases, which you'll read more about in the chapters that follow, the participants have even split between buildings to study what particular initiatives might look like throughout a district or between levels.

Learning Looks. These are quick dips into and out of multiple classrooms. Participants usually travel in smaller groups (pairs or triads), and, as lab hosts, you can plan for a variety of different types of learning looks depending on how structured you'd like their observations to be.

Structured Learning Looks. In structured learning looks, some elements of the schedule are organized ahead of time in order to ensure a more focused or consistent observation experience. To do this, we pre-plan which classrooms participants might visit according to the teachers' schedules and the focus of the lab that day. In one lab that we facilitated, we were studying the first and last 10 minutes of instruction, so we needed to do quite a bit of pre-planning to examine the bell schedules of different middle school teams to give lab participants a specific schedule that would ensure they would see the right classes at the right times. In cases like this, we have found that it's helpful to give participants a map of the building along with a list of classrooms that are available for learning looks during which times.

Unstructured Learning Looks. In this variation, participants have more freedom to choose which classrooms to visit and when. You may use these if you're studying broad topics that span multiple grade levels and/or content areas. In Chapter 5, we describe our process to have teachers post an indicator outside their door if their classroom was available for a visit as one way to facilitate these unstructured learning looks. Another way that we have engaged in these was by communicating with the whole building's staff ahead of the lab to let them know what and why we were learning through the upcoming principal labs. We included the times they might expect to have visitors in their rooms and what they should expect from their visitors while they're there, and we asked that if anyone's classroom was not available for observation (in the case of a test, a substitute teacher, etc.), they respond. You could then let participants know which rooms were off limits by indicating it on a map or by posting a sign outside the classroom door.

Ghost Visits. This type of learning look is one that is done when students aren't present. Rather than watching and listening to what's being done during instruction, participants observe evidence of it (School Reform Initiative, 2017b). Depending on what they're studying, they may make note of bulletin boards, student work, seating arrangement, the whiteboard, and more. We have facilitated true ghost walks where participants examined evidence of a classroom culture, and we've used a hybrid version for learning looks where participants may enter classrooms where students are or are not present.

It's also entirely possible that, within the course of a lab, you might plan for a combination of more than one type of shared observation. In the chapters that follow, we'll explore further how we decide which classes to see and how we time our observations.

Once in the classroom, you may use a variety of observation protocols for participants to collect what they notice in a way that is focused on the day's learning. Through these protocols, participants may observe moves the teachers make, but more important, they should notice what the students say and do during the lesson. John Hattie's (2015) article "High-Impact Leadership" explains that focusing on our instruction's effect on students will have a far greater impact on our overall goal than simply focusing on what the teacher is or is not doing. The particular protocol that you may use for observing and taking notes may vary slightly depending on the type of lab and the participants' lens for learning. Throughout the book, we'll share examples of different approaches to collect observations.

Feedback and Feeding Forward

While it's hard to determine which component of the lab is most important, the time following the observations just might be it. A generous amount of time is devoted to discussing and calibrating on what participants saw in the observations and to make connections to their own buildings. As someone who is planning a lab, this is not the time to present any new material, but rather to facilitate and coach as the participants process what they've experienced. This is a crucial opportunity to reflect on what was observed, make connections to the day's shared experience, and for participants to plan together how to bring the learning back to their buildings. While it's true that in regard to cognitive load, the participants are doing the bulk of the heavy lifting during this time, this can only take place if the time is facilitated with purposeful structures to support the learning. Without tightly facilitated discussion, we've found that you're likely to have administrators sharing notes from their observations that are unrelated to your day's focus or that are rooted in the biases they hold. If principals don't have a strong schema of how instruction differs between secondary and elementary grades, they may focus on aspects that connect with what they know rather than what you hoped they'd notice in the lab. For example, in one early lab that we facilitated, we brought secondary principals to an elementary classroom to observe a writing lesson. We didn't structure this portion of the day intentionally enough, and it became clear when principals wanted to talk more about the posters they saw on the wall and the stories the kids were reading than on the instructional moves that they saw the teacher making. After the lab, we realized that the problem was that principals needed help connecting what they saw in their observation to the instruction they were studying and that we should have done that through facilitation moves in the feedback and feeding forward section of this lab.

We've found a number of helpful structures to plan for facilitation that helps principals engage in a focused way. You may choose to use the following structures to design this portion of the day. In a given lab, the order of these events depends on what makes the most sense for your team and your day's purpose.

Reflection. There is a lot of emphasis on discussion and collaboration throughout principal labs, so it's important to offer some opportunities for participants to process individually throughout the day. You can do this through structured or unstructured prompts for written reflection as well as protocols for pairing individual reflection with small- or whole-group discussions. While it's smart to plan for these individual opportunities at multiple points in the lab, the best time for individual reflection is immediately following an observation. In an observation, there's a lot to take in, especially when you consider that participants are connecting what they see and hear to new learning. Giving everyone a few minutes to quietly unpack their own thinking will ensure that everyone has had the time they need to process before they apply their thinking to a new situation or discussion.

Observation Analysis. Principals are no stranger to observing teachers for evaluations and giving them feedback, but they most often do this nearly, if not entirely, on their own. Observation analysis is a structured discussion to share and learn from each other's thinking while calibrating the observation experience. To help the group stay focused during this discussion, you may choose to use a variety of tools. Sometimes it is as simple as some guiding questions that tie participants' observation notes to the shared experience from earlier in the day. Or, you may choose resources that administrators already use when considering feedback for an observation: rubrics used in teacher evaluation or tools used in your school accreditation process. Regardless of which tools you use, this portion of the lab is designed to unpack what participants saw and heard the students and teachers doing in relation to the overall purpose of the lab.

Data Digs. This is time devoted to collaboratively analyzing relevant data points. The data points that you bring to examine should be driven by the overarching purpose of the lab and what's at the forefront of administrators' consciousness. This is an opportunity to explore questions that bubble up in previous labs or meetings, or to explore data points that have recently been published at the state or local level. To engage in collaborative inquiry, invite participants to examine how the day's learning might connect to this data. This process can help participants stay grounded in analyzing the impact of professional learning and school improvement initiatives.

Collaborative Coaching. This is the section of the lab where the magic really happens! The power doesn't only come from reflecting on what's happening; it comes from planning ahead for next steps that will yield change. And in this planning, collaborative coaching is key. Research on what makes staff development effective shows the need for a combination of studying theory, demonstration, practice, and peer coaching, with the bulk of the load for transfer on coaching (Joyce & Showers, 2002). Coaching helps participants take on and transfer their learning into practice because it gives the participant ownership and decision-making power in a supported way. Because we understand that this ownership is important, we knew that principal labs simply wouldn't work if they felt like another link in a chain of top-down directives. Instead, it was critical to us as we started developing principal labs that we set up experiences that were critical for principals and then facilitated discussion that would help them reflect, draw their own conclusions, and make plans for moving forward. As principals work together in labs, they network to share in each other's expertise and experiences so that they can collaboratively find solutions and take ownership together. Coaching them toward this collaboration is essential because it arms them with some of the most vital tools they'll have as they move outside the lab space and back into their buildings: each other.

Making a Commitment. Without careful attention to the group dynamics and facilitation, it's easy for the feedback and feeding forward section of a lab to feel too critical. For that reason, it's essential to end with reflection that helps participants make concrete what the learning was. We know that it's imperative to build upon appreciative inquiry and ask participants to carry forward the pieces that work well and feel actionable with positive momentum. One way that we've facilitated this was by structuring some reflection questions using the taffy candy Now and Later. We ask the following questions:

- Now: How does your thinking about today's lab tie to what you're working on now?
- Later: How might today's learning influence your work that comes next or later?

You can simply ask everyone to reflect on these questions individually or in table groups. Or, we've also facilitated it through paired discussions by distributing two Now and Later candies to each participant. We then ask them to circulate throughout the room to find someone who has the same color candy as their "now" reflection and to share with each other and then again with a new partner who shares the color as their "later" reflection. This kind of random mixing and sharing can further identify and strengthen connections that might not have been discovered without the lab. This is just one of many variations of reflection activities that you might facilitate, but ultimately, we know that it's important to ask participants some variation of the question "What are you going to do differently tomorrow as a result of spending time together today?" Asking participants to reflect on their experiences in the lab and to identify actionable learning helps principals carry the learning beyond the lab and back into practice.

To begin the work of feedback and feeding forward, invite your team to think through a lens much like a Multi-Tiered System of Support—but for their teachers. In this way, you'll be able to think beyond what verbal or written feedback an administrator might give following an observation and think toward how to plan the next steps to push instruction forward. Joyce and Showers (2002) explain "a structured 'walkthrough' of a planning activity that allows teams to respond to questions within specific time frames provides practice in thinking aloud the things individuals want to accomplish and in identifying the overlap with the agendas of colleagues." Digging into this means that the team should examine how they could work together to intentionally plan for their teachers' needs using structures they already have in place, including

- District-level professional development days.
- Staff meeting times.
- Teacher learning labs.
- Post-observation meetings between teachers and administrators.

We consider this work a form of collaborative coaching because, rather than the lab facilitators outlining a plan for participants to take on, the participants apply their new learning and data gleaned from their observations to determine plans that they want to enact. They should do this in strategic groups that involve members in many roles and capitalize on the networking and relationship building that are central to the design of principal labs.

Responsive Planning

When combined together, the elements of relationship building, an anchoring experience, shared observation, and feedback and feeding forward can create a professional learning opportunity that ensures participants will have the tools and support necessary to carry the learning beyond the day's experience and into their own work (Joyce & Showers, 2002). It is not our intent for the structure of principal labs to seem prescriptive. On the contrary, our greatest hope is that you should read this book and begin planning for principal labs that can fit the needs of your school or district no matter the size or demographics. Within these common elements, we expect that you'll make decisions to plan for a principal lab that is responsive to the needs of your participants. You might think of your planning process in terms of a flowchart (see Figure 2.2) in which you make decisions to tailor each component. Once you've decided how to plan for each element, you'll build the day's agenda to share with your participants (see Figure 2.3).

To guide you in how to plan for these variables, we advise you to always start planning each lab with a pulse of what your participants' biggest need is. What hurdles do they face as instructional leaders? What frustrations do they share? Once you determine what they need, that will shape the purpose of your lab, and you can plan for variation within each of these elements accordingly.

When we first started planning principal labs, we didn't look at each one as a specific type of lab; instead, we assessed the needs of our team and designed individual labs to meet those learning needs. Throughout this process, we realized that some trends were starting to emerge, and we could categorize each lab that we'd facilitated into different types. In Chapters 4–7, we'll help you understand what the elements of principal labs look like through the lens of each of these main types of lab (see Figure 2.4).

In each of those chapters, we'll outline questions to examine while planning each part of the lab, and we'll share with you examples of principal labs that we've run and how we took on those planning questions. Each chapter will start with a sample agenda to give you a frame of

FIGURE 2.2

Structure Flowchart

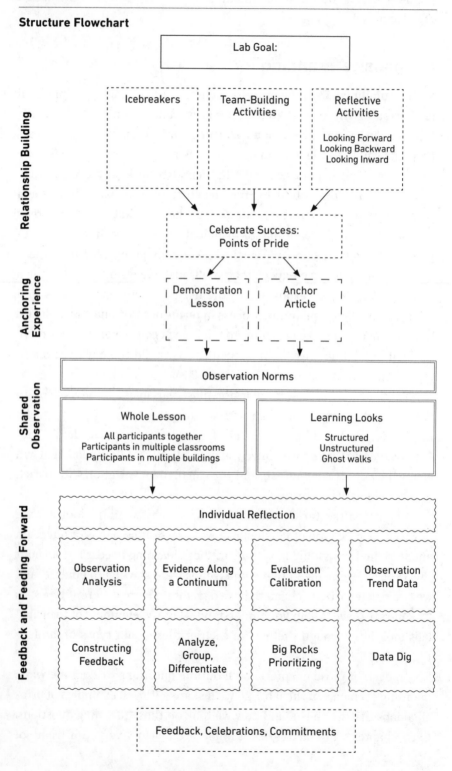

FIGURE 2.3

Principal Lab Agenda

Leading and Learning Through Collaborative Partnerships

Morning

Relationship Building
- Connector
- Points of Pride

Anchoring Experience: Model Lesson or Shared Reading
Shared Observation
Feedback and Feeding Forward
- Individual Reflection
- Observation Analysis

Lunch and Thank-You Notes to Teacher Hosts

Afternoon

Data Dig
Responsive Planning
Reflection
- How will today's experience influence your work in your building tomorrow?

Thinking Ahead
- What additional support could we provide?
- How can we design the next principal lab experience to best meet your learning needs?

Adapted with permission from Waterford School District.

reference for how the day might flow, and then throughout the chapter we'll include samples of note catchers and tools that we use throughout our facilitation. These chapters and their tools are not meant to show you the only way to run a particular type of lab; rather, they're meant to help you see inside our planning and facilitation so you can begin to plan for a lab that may fit similar needs for your team.

Chapter 8 will then explore some logistical moves that we find helpful in planning all principal labs— no matter what type. Following Chapter 8, you'll find what we call the "clipboard." Whenever we facilitate a principal lab, a clipboard is one of our most essential tools. While you may use our clipboard materials and ideas to get you started, we hope that you'll adapt the resources and facilitation to make principal labs a structure for professional learning that will fit the unique and changing needs of the principals you work with.

FIGURE 2.4

Types of Labs

Lab Purpose	Focus	Target	Shared Observations
Labs to Introduce New Curriculum (Chapter 4)	Curriculum implementation	Administrators will learn how to best support their teachers as they implement new curriculum.	Span several classrooms in one building and study how to support the risks teachers are taking.
Labs to Study Instructional Practices (Chapter 5)	Instructional best practice	Administrators will analyze teachers' current instructional practices and collaborate on how to best support teachers along the continuum.	Study exemplar teacher/student examples of high-yield instructional practice and learning looks to gauge where teachers are in relation to the target.
Labs to Build a Network of Leaders (Chapter 6)	Strengthen improvement efforts by empowering and leveraging key leaders	Leaders and administrators will study classrooms to learn and collaboratively plan for how to support improvement efforts in their own buildings.	Study current practices within and across a system (building, district, or ISD).
Labs to Foster Collaborative Aspirations (Chapter 7)	Network around the study of a self-selected topic that is relevant and timely to their current work	Administrators will work in collaborative partnerships to study, discuss, and support a problem of practice.	Include the study of practices within specific buildings across the system.

3

Laying the Groundwork

Although the principal lab structure has consistent elements, it is about so much more than plugging components into an agenda and pushing play. Since the labs are a mechanism for deep, collaborative work, a culture for learning and leadership is essential.

Probably because of this, we've found that, when we share our principal lab work with others, they're sometimes skeptical. If that collaborative culture isn't perfectly in place, administrators sometimes have difficulty imagining labs taking hold in their district, but that doesn't have to be the case.

You don't have to have perfect conditions to begin principal labs; indeed, thoughtful structuring and facilitation can help solve some of the problems you may be facing. For example, when we first started getting serious about developing the learning lab structure for principals, it was largely because we felt like we weren't as collaborative as we needed to be. Yes, we recognized the need for curriculum and instruction support for principals, but mostly, we knew we needed to get everyone talking to each other. Each building in the district felt a little like an island. We spent a lot more time and energy planning around the relationship-building components for our first few principal labs, and it paid off. Soon, principals were reaching out to each other and to central office staff with questions like "Hey, I heard about that summer reading program you're doing. Can you tell me more about that?" That collaborative culture is essential for the success of principal labs. We didn't have it firmly in place before we started; instead, we consciously built it through our labs.

In order to be able to troubleshoot, build the culture we needed, and run principal labs that offered meaningful learning for participants, we realized that we were designing labs with a set of shared beliefs that run throughout all of our decision making. These are the beliefs that we hold, and some of the choices that we've made in service of those, that have helped us make principal labs successful for us. Whether you've got a lot of this in place already or you want to problem solve through the use of principal labs, keeping these beliefs at the core of your planning can help make principal labs a structure for professional learning that is impactful for you and your colleagues.

We believe that a shared vision is fundamental.

When it comes to teaching and learning, it's easy to take this for granted. We can sometimes think that we all got into this for the same reasons, we're all in the trenches together, and so we all must "get it." While this may be possible from a broad perspective, the reality is that we are all coming to the table with our own unique experiences. Take mental stock of your administrative team for a minute: Did they teach before their current role? What level or classes? When? Even at this very surface-level reflection, we expect you'd find a wide variety of experiences. We believe that there is great value in this diversity of experience, but it also underscores the need to explicitly work together toward a shared vision.

Slowing down to have conversations and establish a common vision is some of the most valuable time you can take as a team. In *Collaborative Inquiry for Educators,* Jenni Donohoo (2013) explains that doing visioning work "will help the team determine where they are, where they want to go, and how to get there. The purpose of these activities is to ensure that the team shares a clear vision of what success looks like and sounds like" (pp. 16–17). Once everyone has the same understanding of these success criteria, they can move forward into daily work. Fullan and Quinn (2016) describe this as the "glue" that will keep together the coherence of your team. And Harshak and others (2010) explain from the business world, that this visioning work shapes "the fabric of the organization." However you choose to describe it, carving out time to explore and construct your group's shared vision will shape how you do business every day.

If you're reading this right now and thinking that you've done visioning work that didn't have this impact or that was a waste of time, chances are good you've been involved in visioning work gone wrong: perhaps it was quickly constructed or merely cosmetic in nature. In her book *Onward,* about cultivating a culture of resilience for educators, coaching and leadership expert Elena Aguilar (2018) explains that having a shared purpose is not only vital, but also that it is important for this work to be rooted in participants' core values. Core values can change over time and vary widely within even a seemingly homogenous group, so it's important to do work to lift and live into the shared values. Aguilar explains how rooting visioning work in values can make the work more authentic and intrinsic: "People want to feel connected to values and connected to each other through values. When shared values aren't strong, people resort to their own individual values, which weakens the school's overall mission" (p. 25).

And it will pay off in the long run. Fullan and Sharratt (2007) note that a "condition for sustainability involves working on defining, shaping, and refining the shared vision of the school" (p. 127). Having these conversations as you start your work together will give you more leverage to lean into the work in the beginning, shape how you live into it daily, and ultimately make space for learning and change that will last.

We believe principal labs exist within a system for professional learning.

If you're looking for significant results in your student data or in instruction, installing principal labs on their own probably won't do much for you. Principal labs do, indeed, provide valuable learning for instructional leaders, which is undoubtedly impactful, but if the role of an instructional leader is to support those facilitating the instruction, then there must be a system in place (or under construction) for supporting those classroom instructors.

When we first started working together, we began developing a system for professional learning that would stick. To do this, we combined our understanding of Multi-Tiered Systems of Support (MTSS) and the work of Hattie, Fisher, Frey, and others (2017) on surface, deep, and transfer learning to construct a system for professional learning. We thought about our content, structure, and audience for our professional learning opportunities. In *Visible Learning for Mathematics,* Hattie and colleagues explain student learning:

> What and when are equally important when it comes to instruction that has an impact on learning. Approaches that facilitate students' surface-level learning do not work equally well for deep learning, and vice versa. Matching the right approach with the appropriate phase of learning is the critical lesson to be learned. (p. 9)

We believe that this thinking applies to adult learners as well, so we built our professional learning plans by thinking about who needs what content and support and when.

We took this understanding and made connections to MTSS in order to guide us toward being responsive in a systemic way. This helped us plan for surface learning and support of application through learning labs, collaboratively scored student work, and one-on-one coaching. Principals already participated in surface-level learning alongside their teachers, and they discussed plans regularly through administrative and school improvement meetings. But we realized that we didn't have a professional learning structure in place for principals to be vulnerable with each other as they began applying new learning and discussing what it might mean for them as instructional leaders.

An interconnected systems-based approach is outlined throughout Learning Forward's Standards for Professional Learning. In the introduction to their workbook to support creating a professional learning system, Joellen Killion (2013) explains:

> A comprehensive professional learning system has essential components, but how those components operate in each context will vary. Excluding some of the components or designing them so they are ill fitting may mean that the efficiency and reliability of the system will fail sooner or later. (p. 4)

Once we began incorporating principal labs as a targeted way to help administrators apply new learning, it was impactful. We knew that it wouldn't have been as powerful without the other pieces of the system in place, and we knew that those other pieces weren't as significant without the principal labs there. In the truest sense of the meaning of the word "system," principal labs are one mechanism, interconnected and dependent on the others. Principal labs are the glue that made all other professional learning stick throughout the system.

We believe that our own learning is valuable.

It's too easy for leaders to put themselves second. Aren't we told, so often, that this is a good thing when it comes to leadership? Lead from behind, lift others up, prioritize others' needs. Those sound noble, but when it comes to professional learning, applying that mindset at face value is misguided. When there's money (or time) set aside for professional development, building leaders tend to prioritize their teachers and put their own learning on the back burner. While that may indeed be well-intentioned, it's a little bit like the oxygen mask theory. You know, the one that says that if an airplane were to experience an emergency, you must first put an oxygen mask on yourself so that you'll be able to help others with theirs? When applying this theory to professional learning, leaders should put on their own oxygen masks first before they can guide others in their learning. Doing so not only makes leaders more effective— it models the desired culture for learning. Fullan and Quinn (2016) call this being the "lead learner." Now, we're not arguing that you must do all the learning first before your teachers, but we do believe that, as a leader, you should recognize that your own learning can make you better able to lead others.

Believing your own learning is valuable and making time for it in an otherwise packed schedule can be two separate feats, though. We've found that, beyond communicating our beliefs about the importance of learning for learners, we could get participants to buy into learning time being valuable if we also made steps to recognize that their time is valuable through thoughtful scheduling. This can mean looking at the big picture and purposefully scheduling principal labs at key times through-out the year, giving multiple options for dates participants can attend, and being mindful of the minutes within the day by giving grace time and scheduled breaks for participants to attend to some of the daily business of their jobs. In Chapter 8, we'll detail some specific examples of ways to honor their time within the principal lab structure.

We believe there is great power in collaborative inquiry and its inherent vulnerability.

It might seem contradictory to say that there is power in vulnerability, but we believe that creating a culture where the "courage to get curious" and "rumble with vulnerability," as Brené Brown (2018) puts it in her book *Dare to Lead,* is not only valued but vital. She explains, "Building the grounded confidence to rumble with vulnerability and discomfort rather than armoring up, running away, shutting down, or tapping out, completely prepares you for living into your values, building trust, and learning to rise" (p. 166). Living into this establishes a culture that wholly values learning—the ultimate goal of a highly functioning school—and it works to build trust among colleagues, which is a crucial underpinning to a truly collaborative relationship.

Indeed, the practice is crucial for building leadership, but it's a sound practice to deepen and sustain professional learning, too. In their book studying a framework for professional learning for disciplinary literacy, Dobbs, Ippolito, and Charner-Laird (2017) explain, "Recent research has found that professional learning that includes teachers working together over extended periods of time around shared problems of practice is more likely to lead to meaningful changes in practice than single-session, one-stop professional development workshops" (p. 34). And if that's true for teachers, the same could be said for all educators—especially those in leadership. There is great power in showing up and saying, "I don't have all the answers, but I want to learn more, and I want to do it with you."

Embracing the vulnerability inherent in digging into problems and the unknown establishes a culture for learning that goes deeper than any surface-level learning could, and extending this culture outward toward the leadership will not only ensure deeper learning on their part but also establish a culture for learning that is systemic.

We believe that all participants are valuable and that their voices need to be heard.

Anyone who has ever facilitated professional learning knows that it's most likely to fall flat if it feels like something that's being done *to* its participants rather than *for* or *with* its participants. We've found that, in order for participants to really feel as though the professional learning is there as a resource and support for them, they need to know that their experiences, cultures, and backgrounds; needs; and unique strengths are valued. In any school or district, the power dynamics of an administrative team are complex. It is not unusual for racial, gender, cultural, or other biases to lead to an "old boys' club" dynamic that can produce inequitable representation of necessary voices and opinions in the room. In order to begin to disrupt this status quo and move into inclusive and vulnerable learning that will truly move the school or district, it is up to the team to take deliberate facilitation steps to ensure that everyone's contributions are valued. Only then will all participants trust the experience enough to open up and be vulnerable with their own learning.

Brown (2018) explains that trust toward vulnerability is built through the accumulation of many small interactions. For that reason, we know that building a culture in which participants believe their voice is valued is not something that's done with any one opening activity or regurgitated statement. Instead, it's woven throughout many actions intentionally planned for in each lab experience. This can often be done in subtle and nuanced ways, but we consistently include taking time to celebrate successes, collaboratively establishing working agreements, intentionally utilizing discussion protocols, and continuously gathering feedback to inform our planning. In the chapters that follow, we'll detail some of the specific ways we planned for each of these in various types of labs.

Moving from Beliefs into Practice

When we first started to play with the idea of principal labs, they were OK—but just that: OK. We borrowed the format from well-established teacher learning labs, but the principal labs felt a little like we were just going through the motions without any real momentum. We knew the learning lab structure effectively supported teachers in our building, so we built principal labs that mirrored that structure. But, while we knew that principals needed professional learning targeted toward their unique needs as instructional leaders, we didn't initially recognize the many ways in which their roles made this more complex. For example, teachers were used to regularly attending professional learning throughout the year, but for many of the principals we worked with, that expectation was new, and they felt anxious at the idea of being out of their building for a whole day and thus had a hard time concentrating. We realized that, though how we structured the day may be largely the same, how we approached labs with principals would need to adapt.

As we started to get more serious about making the labs a part of our professional learning system, we leaned in more to our shared beliefs. Through planning, trial and error, and ultimately rumbling with our own vulnerability, we learned that we believe

- A shared vision is fundamental.
- Principal labs exist within a system for professional learning.
- Our own learning is valuable.
- There is great power in collaborative inquiry and its inherent vulnerability.
- All participants are valuable, and their voices need to be heard.

Once we named these beliefs that run throughout successful principal lab implementation, we were able to identify some of the obstacles that got in the way. What follows are some of the approaches we identified to help us to put our beliefs into practice so that we could navigate the inevitable obstacles and continue to grow principal labs into a high-leverage learning opportunity rooted in shared beliefs designed specifically for principals.

Embracing Being an Instructional Leader

Although most principals we've worked with say being an instructional leader is part of their identity as an administrator, we strongly suspect that, if they were to design a pie chart detailing how they spent their time each week, they'd find that they were having trouble making time for the actions inherent to being an instructional leader. Taking the time to participate in professional learning and plan for supporting others in their learning is no easy feat when so many other tasks can quickly demand priority in a principal's daily schedule. For many principals, being able to close the laptop or ignore the emails for a few hours and actually participate in a professional learning session with their teachers seems like a huge win.

To be sure, actively participating in professional learning alongside your teachers is a win for an instructional leader, but principal labs put the role of instructional leader front and center in a principal's identity—not something that you make time for occasionally if the scheduling stars align. When principal labs are connected to teacher professional learning, school improvement planning, staff meetings, and PLCs, you'll likely find that activities devoted to instructional leadership will take up a much bigger slice of your pie chart. In order to help principals embrace this shifting identity, we've found that there are no quick and easy ways to flip the switch and suddenly take on a new mindset. Rather, it's done through subtle, repeated acts that can be supported within the structure of a principal lab and alongside it.

A district that we were working with held two large professional development days a year. On those days, teachers had their choice of several sessions to attend, and we noticed that principals' participation in these days varied greatly. While a few took on instructional leadership so fully that they facilitated sessions, some traveled to some choice sessions, and others prioritized other work instead. To help all principals realize their leadership roles within these days, prior to the scheduled day, we shared the schedule with all principals and asked them to reflect on two major questions:

1. Which sessions do you plan to attend?
2. How will you follow up or continue the day's learning in your building?

To plan for some professional development days, we found that we could facilitate this conversation at the end of a preceding principal lab, and for others, this conversation happened at an administrative team meeting or through an email.

Another way we worked to help principals more fully take on the role of instructional leader was to shift the act of evaluation from being a task to giving feedback. Much like the shift in education where teachers move away from assigning summative marks to instead give ongoing feedback for continuous growth, we felt the need to shift the assessment culture within the administrative team. For many principals, teacher evaluations can feel like a task to be completed rather than an authentic component in a system for supporting growth. This is one reason why the feedback and feeding forward portion of a principal lab is such a critical part of the day. It moves the learning space out of simply seeing what's happening toward strategizing for how to react in smaller, individual feedback interactions and in larger, systemic planning for professional learning. We also found that the observation component of principal labs can be a mechanism for getting principals into classrooms more regularly, which is critical for moving the evaluation observations out of the checkbox mentality of completing an evaluation and into an authentic cycle for feedback. When a principal only observes a classroom once or twice a year for formal observations, it's common for teachers to want to put on their best face and plan for a lesson to show off. In this way, what the principal observes and gives feedback on is not authentic. Because in the lesson teachers are trying to showcase their best, when a principal offers a critique, it feels like a demerit rather than a supportive nudge forward. This is something that can be equally frustrating for a principal who wants to embrace cycles of authentic observation and support but has trouble getting to the level of trust and vulnerability needed for that to occur.

When principals visit classrooms more frequently for nonevaluative visits—and even for shorter periods of time like with learning looks—it becomes a more natural part of the teachers' instructional experience, and principals are therefore more likely to see what teachers are really working on. And, although most principals carve out time on their calendars to build this culture through walkthroughs, most also recognize that when the phone starts ringing and more urgent matters start piling up, those walkthroughs can be hard to fit in. Offering sheltered time through principal labs can give principals the opportunity to get back some of the informal observation time they want to prioritize.

It's worth noting here that this is built into every level of a district's assessment culture. Just as we're describing how principals should offer ongoing formative feedback like teachers should formatively assess, it's important to also examine how this culture plays out in principals' own evaluation systems. Do the principals in your district get feedback that helps them grow along a clearly articulated continuum, or does it feel like a formality or a stamp of approval at the end of the school year? This vertical alignment throughout the system is one reason we've discovered it's so critical to invite central office administrators to your principal labs alongside your building-level administrators.

Busting Competition and Building Collaboration

Whether the principals in your labs come from schools that are cross-town rivals or schools that vie for scores and enrollment, it's likely that some participants will bring an element of competition to your labs—at least in the beginning. This can be a tough obstacle to tackle. If a principal perceives that their own staff must in some way outperform the teachers from another building, they're not as likely to be vulnerable about opening up their building's classrooms for growth, and they're a lot more likely to shift into a critical space when visiting buildings that aren't their own. Much like with any shift in culture, we've found that addressing this problem isn't something that happens with one conversation or activity; rather, it shifts along with your culture through the facilitation of your labs and the ways in which you connect the labs to other pieces of your instructional system.

Moving away from a competitive administrative culture goes hand in hand with the shift away from assessment and toward growth. If principals see evaluations as a mark of a job well done rather than evidence of growth along a continuum, it's likely that shift away from an assessment-centered culture will also affect any competitive subculture. When the culture prioritizes feedback and learning over assessment and evaluation, principals can shift into a collaborative space. Throughout all aspects of education, we know that learning is a social endeavor, and we encourage it in our students and our teachers.

Because this obstacle involves complexities and dynamics that will range from building to building and between individual personalities, we recognize that it's not as simple as saying that once you shift principals into a space of learning, the competitiveness will dissolve. This is one reason why we believe so strongly in spending time during each lab to connect and celebrate points of pride among all participants. These small acts, built up over time, can have lasting effects on building the relationships needed to embrace the social nature of labs and engage in collaboration rather than competition.

Generating Interest and Curiosity Among Principals

If you're going to ask your colleagues to spend considerable time with you shifting how they identify within their role as a principal, it has to be something they want to do. Generating interest for principal labs isn't about whiz-bang marketing or incentivizing the process with external motivation. Instead, we found that it was critical to believe that principal labs exist within a larger system for professional learning and that our own learning is valuable. Staying rooted in these beliefs as we made daily decisions about how to facilitate labs and what professional learning system best connects with the labs helped us make principal labs feel purposeful, which is key to developing the intrinsic motivation that authentically generates interest. Some of those smaller decisions include connecting the labs to

- Administrative staff meetings.
- School improvement team meetings and work.
- Professional learning at a district and building level.
- Principals' own goals for their growth and progress.
- Areas of growth identified in state or local data points.

We made these connections largely in our planning process. For example, if in an administrative staff meeting, principals examined their recently released standardized test scores and developed some questions and hypotheses, we planned to dig further into their inquiry in a subsequent principal lab. Or, if a central office leader recognized that many principals had similar personal growth goals through their own evaluation cycles, we planned for principal labs that would provide support in those areas. Or, as you'll read about more in Chapter 4, when teachers in a district were adopting a new curriculum resource and were deeply engaged in professional learning around it, principals in those buildings quickly realized that they needed a chance to learn more about it themselves, so we planned a lab to introduce new curriculum to help them navigate the questions they were getting from parents and teachers alike. Keeping the content of the principal labs connected to their needs, their role, and the rest of their learning systems helped generate interest in an authentically engaging way.

Generating Interest and Curiosity Among Teachers

Principal labs are focused on the principals' learning in the labs, but because the day involves getting into teachers' classrooms, you can't ignore how the teachers in your building are feeling. If you're going to ask them to allow a bunch of administrators to come stand around the edges of their classrooms, clipboards in hand, and watch them teach, you're going to need to get teachers on board by generating their own interest and curiosity in the labs. Much like developing authentic and intrinsic motivation is key with the principals involved, the same is true of teachers. And, in much the same way, keeping the principal labs connected to other aspects of professional learning will be key in getting teachers interested.

Tying the content of principal labs to the focus of teachers' professional learning is perhaps the most effective way to generate interest from teaching staff. We realized, when facilitating teacher labs where teachers were taking on new practices, they would say things like "Yeah, but does my principal know this?" The sentiment stemmed from the idea that teachers were engaged in their own professional learning and risk taking, but they were nervous to make changes because they worried that their administrators would only see the messiness that is inherent in changing practice. Framing principal labs as a way to help principals understand the hard work teachers are taking on in professional learning makes their risk taking an investment that's worth it.

To help teachers see this connection, communication is key. It may come from the teachers' own building principals during walkthrough and observation cycles. Principal labs work to build administrators' vulnerability as lead learners, and if they ask questions like "What should I learn about in order to better support you in this area?" the reflection following an observation is much more likely to be authentic and grounded in mutual learning. In Chapter 4, we'll also detail a reflective protocol we've asked teachers to use during the course of their professional learning that we share with principals in the lab so that they can better understand the teachers' experiences and needs for support firsthand. Oftentimes, these facilitated reflections or general exit tickets that ask teachers to finish a prompt like "the one thing your principal needed to understand one thing about this learning" build the culture of learning and growth and facilitate dialogue between principals and teachers about their learning.

Disconnecting Evaluations and Observations

In every principal lab you facilitate, you'll engage in some kind of observation. If, in a building, the word "observation" is synonymous with "evaluation," you may find that you have a problem—both for the principals in your lab and for the teachers in their buildings. If the only time administrators ever observe teacher instruction is during a formal observation, teachers are likely to be nervous and less likely to let principals observe their authentic instruction. Likewise, you don't want principals who participate in the labs to conflate any of their lab observation experiences with formal evaluations and carry over anything that they saw or discussed in a punitive way.

In order for principal labs to take off, you need to work on ensuring that teachers aren't afraid of having principals visit their classrooms. This comes down to four intentional moves: clearly communicating the intent and purpose of the observation and its related learning, connecting to systems for professional learning, increasing the frequency of classroom observations, and operating in an asset-based stance.

Clearly communicating the purpose of your principal lab with all teachers will help set their minds at ease. In Chapter 8, we'll share some logistics and specifics regarding what and how you might want to share the lab's details with teachers, but the bottom line is that it's important to be proactive and transparent about your goal with the lab and your observation. At the minimum, it's critical to explain to teachers that principal labs are designed to help principals learn to better support their teachers and explicitly state that the lab observations are in no way tied to any part of their evaluations. We've also found that it can be helpful in some cases to share more details with the host teachers about what principals will be learning in the lab. If, for example, the principals will be anchoring their lab's learning in an article, also sharing the article with the host teachers can help them understand the focus of the learning and move the observation out of the realm of evaluation in their minds. In Chapter 5, we'll also explain how we used a tool to collaborate between principals in the lab and teachers in their building to determine look-fors along an instructional continuum. Because teachers had a say in what principals would be looking for, they saw the connection between their own learning and the principals' learning.

Similarly, it's important to believe that principals are just one component within a system of professional learning. If the focus of a principal lab is the same as the professional learning sessions and learning labs you've facilitated with teachers, there won't be any surprises, and it's much easier to explain to teachers what their principals will be learning when they observe their class during a principal lab. If the principal lab is the principal's version of what teachers have been experiencing and engaging with, it feels like a more natural fit and a complementary component of a strong professional learning system that is based on continual collaborative growth and improvement.

As we shift the culture to feedback over evaluation, getting into more classrooms more frequently is key. If the only time teachers see a principal in their room is during formal evaluations, it's going to ramp up the stress level even further when several principals come to observe during a principal lab. The observations and learning looks within the principal labs themselves can certainly help shift this culture and get more administrators into classrooms more frequently, but we found that we worked to shift this habit outside and alongside principal labs as well. For example, when we first started to authentically connect the school improvement process within a district's system for professional learning, we asked building principals to do walkthroughs with members of their school improvement committee. These functioned more like an informal version of instructional rounds than a principal lab, but we asked them to visit several classrooms for short amounts of time at least three times a year to get a taste for how their building incorporated the school improvement plan. Although there was good discussion and appreciative inquiry, we believe that the real power in this practice was in making it a more common occurrence for principals to walk in and out of teachers' rooms in ways that were completely unrelated to their formal evaluations.

Throughout your observations, whether they are shared, whole-class observations or quick dips into multiple classrooms through learning looks, it's important to focus principals in an asset-based stance. Although in analysis you're sure to identify problems to solve collaboratively, when you go into a classroom, it's critical to focus on what you do see happening rather than on what you don't see or what's wrong. This will set you up for appreciative inquiry, which will help your group create a collaborative culture, and it will help classroom observations take on a growth focus.

Planning and Prioritizing Principal Labs

Asking a principal to be out of their buildings for an entire day multiple times a year for the sole purpose of their own professional learning can be a hard sell. There are no two ways around that. But this is deeply tied to our belief about our own learning being valuable. Yes, other urgent matters will come up in your building, but it can be a critical step forward to recognize that, sometimes, what's important needs to take priority over what's urgent (Covey, Merrill, & Merrill, 1995). As we plan the schedule for principal labs, we must intentionally build in time for some of those urgent matters through periodic breaks and flexible date choices so that building administrative teams can stagger when they are out of the building. We'll explain in more detail some of the logistics around these scheduling decisions in Chapter 8.

Managing the Messiness

Any building principal is sure to feel that the saying about best laid plans going awry was written with them in mind. With one phone call, your day's schedule can look drastically different before first period classes even get started. It would be silly to ignore this fact while designing professional learning for principals. We found that it was helpful to name this throughout the labs, to acknowledge to our colleagues that we were thankful they gave us their time, that we understood how messy their schedules can get, and that they sometimes might need to prioritize something at their building. When you're facilitating professional learning that takes a whole day, extending grace to your participants helps them understand that you value their time. Because you value their time and their presence, they may also feel a value for your time together in professional learning.

Aside from acknowledging the messiness of a principal's daily schedule and extending grace, it can also be helpful to have some norming conversations in your early labs that help principals make decisions about how they navigate it. You can do this by asking participants to name the many things that typically interrupt the flow of their regularly scheduled work days. They might come up with a list that includes things like parent phone calls, discipline referrals, injuries, inclement weather calls, and more. Once they've brainstormed, ask them to categorize those interruptions according to how they might handle each:

- Wait until after the lab.
- Deal with this during a scheduled break.
- Another administrator or substitute administrator in the building can handle this.
- Emergency—step out as needed.

This categorization can help principals in your lab recognize that not every email filling their inbox is an emergency, and it reaffirms that you understand their time is valuable and that they are making adjustments to be in the lab with you. What's more, deciding when others in the building might take over can help administrators recognize that they are part of a team and not always left to manage the messiness on their own.

Visioning the Lab Itself

Once you've made the time and gotten everyone in a room together, sharing ownership about how the labs will run can help everyone recognize the time as valuable. In some of our early labs, we carved out time at the beginning of the day to chart out what everyone wanted to learn together both during that day and beyond, and then we asked how they wanted to learn. We again charted their answers to keep ourselves rooted in the conversation throughout the day. Principals lifted hopes like "I want to see how X building is handling this" or "I've heard that the middle school is trying X, and I want to learn more about that." They also wanted time to plan together for their staff and PLC meetings. We then made sure to return to our charts at the end of the lab to reflect on how we did with what we laid out at the beginning of the day, and we circled or starred items that were their hopes for next time. As our lab series progressed, we additionally sometimes reached out to participating principals with surveys to get their feedback on what was valuable time and to help us prioritize the content and focus. Because we had principals help shape how we envisioned our time together, they felt some ownership and could share in the beliefs on which our principal lab foundation is built.

Laying the Groundwork as You Go

It's hard to imagine any district has all of the pieces of a culture in place to implement a series of principal labs instantly and successfully without any bumps along the way. And it's unrealistic to think that you will work to establish all of the elements of your belief before you run your first principal lab. Because any obstacles that you may encounter in engaging principals in sustained, job-embedded professional learning will likely not be simple fixes, it's OK and expected that you'll work to address them throughout your principal labs. As with any learning, sometimes in our principal lab facilitation, we found that we'd make great strides forward only to run into an old familiar stumbling block again. When this happens, we've found that it helps to reflect on our beliefs, in particular where we may be noticing a disconnect, and to then identify which of the many complexities of a principal's role might be contributing to that disconnect. With this understanding and continuous reflection throughout your lab planning process, we are confident that you can lay the groundwork for successful principal labs and a culture of learning for all of your instructional leaders.

FIGURE 4.1

Curriculum Sample Agenda

Principal Lab Agenda
Math Curriculum Adoption

Morning

Relationship Building
- Points of Pride: Share one thing that you are proud is going well in your building.
- Candy Connector: Risks We've Taken

Anchoring Experience: What is our new math curriculum?
- Why New? Why Now?
- Setting the Vision: Curriculum Essentials Article
- Supporting Teacher Struggle (GIVE)

Shared Observation
- Pre-Observation Norms
- Classroom Observations
  - Room 134
  - Room 135
  - Room 137
  - Room 139

- Post-Observation Personal Reflection

Lunch

Afternoon

Feedback and Feeding Forward
- Mixed-Group Discussion: What risks did you see taken?
- Whole-Group Discussion: Connect to GIVE

  - Read and Learn: Giving Feedback
  - Debrief with GIVE and Danielson Domain 2

- Observation Group Discussion: Calibrating Feedback

  - Feedback Notes for Hosts

Reflection
- How will today's experience influence your work in your building tomorrow?

Thinking Ahead
- What other support do you need?
- How can we design the next principal lab experience to best meet your learning needs?

Adapted with permission from Waterford School District.

4

Labs to Introduce New Curriculum

In our experience planning principal labs, we've found that the vast majority of our lab types study either new curriculum or instruction. And that's natural—curriculum and instruction are both at the heart of what goes on in the classroom. So, if they are so intertwined, why study them separately? The answer lies in the need for support—both for the administrators and the teachers in your district or school. If your teachers' need for support spans across content areas and in many different settings, it's likely that tapping into how to give feedback centered on instruction is going to yield the greatest results for you as an instructional leader. But, if the need is concentrated into one content area and stems from the adoption of new curricula or standards, then the type of support should be more focused. That's where labs to introduce new curriculum come in.

We know that the path to the principalship is a varied one. Administrators come from a variety of teaching experiences and content areas, and if they are to take on the role of instructional leadership, it is crucial that they build expertise in an increased scope of content areas. In their 2003 study titled "Leadership Content Knowledge," Mary Kay Stein and Barbara S. Nelson suggest that administrators "develop expertise in other subjects by 'postholing,' that is, conducting in-depth explorations of an important but bounded slice of the subject, how it is learned, and how it is taught. The purpose of postholing is to learn how knowledge

45

is built in that subject, what learning tasks should look like, and what good instruction looks like" (p. 446). Labs to introduce new curriculum provide administrators of all levels the opportunity to develop this content understanding in the context of the new curriculum.

The key to any successful lesson lies in the planning that goes into it, and principal labs are no exception. We have provided some key questions we used when planning for each portion of a lab to introduce new curriculum.

Determining Focus

How should you approach the focus of supporting a new curriculum?

Most new curriculum adoption processes involve a lot of stakeholders from students to school board members, but ultimately, teachers are the ones who will determine the success of the curriculum implementation, and it is their administrators' job to ensure that each teacher has the best opportunity to implement successfully with support and quality feedback. This is a huge responsibility for both the teachers and their principals.

When you walk into the classroom of a teacher who is taking on new curriculum, it can be tough to recognize what's new and what might be causing a teacher to feel off balance, and that can make it hard to support them. When teachers are adopting new curriculum, it's safe to have the working assumption that they feel vulnerable—and it's likely their whole PLC (or system of support) is in the same boat. Without systematic support, you run the risk of teachers falling back into previous, more comfortable practices while never fully embracing the new curriculum.

In his book *Embarrassment,* Thomas Newkirk (2017) explains what he calls the awkwardness principle: "any act of learning requires us to suspend a natural tendency to want to appear fully competent. We need to accept the fact that we will be awkward, that our first attempts at a new skill will, at best, be only partial successes. Moreover we need to allow this awkwardness to be viewed by some mentor who can offer feedback as we open ourselves up for instruction" (p. 10). When an entire PLC is at the same stage of curriculum implementation, they're all feeling the same awkwardness principle, which makes it hard for them to mentor each other. So when their evaluator enters the classroom, their mentorship is crucial. The feedback they give has the potential to either strengthen the teacher's confidence or break it entirely. Even the most well-intentioned piece of feedback may not take into account the vulnerability or awkwardness the teacher is feeling, and it could be enough to make the teacher throw their hands up and say, "That's it. This just doesn't work. I'm going back to what I was doing before."

Add to this scenario the fact that the content and curriculum are also new to the evaluators, so they're feeling similar vulnerabilities. It's just as likely for principals to want to retreat to what they know or feel comfortable giving feedback on, which we've found usually tends to lean toward classroom management. This is where labs to introduce new curriculum come in.

We recognized a need for this type of lab when a district we were working with adopted new curriculum for their Algebra I classes. The rollout was anticipated to be challenging compared to the recent adoption of curriculum materials for other content areas. This was largely because the new curriculum required a significant shift in instructional style for most of the teachers involved. Teachers had decided on the curriculum as a group, and, through research on effective instructional methods, they knew it was the best decision for their students. Still, they were scared. Their traditional norms of teaching were being challenged. This was an extremely fragile time in the change process. Any feedback from an evaluative administrator that hinted at wrongdoing could bring their momentum to a standstill—or worse, cause them to retreat.

We realized that it was imperative to bring administrators together to better learn how to support their teachers during this critical time, so we began planning a lab to introduce them to the new algebra curriculum.

What content areas are implementing new curriculum or standards?

You might feel like this should go without saying. But it's worth making visible where each content area is in the curriculum adoption process. It's entirely possible that, when you hear the words "new curriculum," a particular PLC already pops into your head. That PLC is probably the obvious choice for a lab to introduce new curriculum, but it's also possible that it's simply the most comfortable being vocal about it. Every PLC or department has its own dynamics and personalities, and some make their discomfort known while others tend to hide it. Sometimes the loudest department is loud for a reason: they're desperately in need of support. But make sure you have the whole picture in front of you as you begin to consider whether any labs to introduce new curriculum are necessary.

When you encounter a department that is reaching out for support or in frustration with their new curriculum, you may ask some reflective questions to determine if a principal lab to introduce new curriculum would be helpful. Some of these questions include

- How involved have building principals been in the rollout and associated training with this new curriculum?
- How comfortable do principals feel in determining ways in which this new curriculum is similar to and different from the previous one?
- How comfortable do principals feel giving feedback to their teachers around this new curriculum?
- How comfortable do building administrators feel fielding questions about the new curriculum from parents and the community?

Asking these questions can help determine if administrator support in the form of a principal lab, as in Figure 4.1, is a helpful next step or if the teachers need additional layers of support for themselves.

It's also entirely possible that there are departments in your building who have not been as forthcoming in expressing their discomfort with a new resource, and they can be overshadowed by those who are. To help determine if this may be the case, you may visually lay out a timeline for each PLC that is grappling with a new curriculum to see where they are in the adoption process. This can help shine a light on content areas that may have a much newer curriculum but have not been vocal about asking for support so that you and your administration team can take a more proactive approach.

What about the new curriculum is different from the previous one, and how much instructional support is required?

If the differences are small, it's unlikely you'll need a lab. You could learn to support these teachers by attending professional learning sessions alongside them, participating in a PLC with them, or conferring with them throughout the observation process. If the differences have deeper instructional implications, though, then a lab to study this might be a perfect fit.

For example, when we were considering possible labs for a new algebra or civics curriculum, we recognized that both required teachers to use more collaboration in their instruction. The district already had several opportunities established for teachers and administrators to share in professional learning around building collaborative cultures and practices in their classrooms, so we determined that principals didn't need a lab to help them support their civics teachers; they felt comfortable doing so with the resources already in place. The new algebra curriculum, however, not only integrated more collaboration but shifted from a product focus to a process focus. Instead of students learning the math and then attempting to apply it to story problems at the end of a unit, the new curriculum engaged them in real-world applications from the first day of instruction. Everything from seating arrangements to homework procedures to lesson design would look different.

To add to that newness, one of the high school buildings had seen a considerable and unexpected turnover in math teachers in between the time the new curriculum was piloted and adopted. And, although a few of the building administrators had taught math previously, the process focus was new for them as well, and they weren't sure what to say when a teacher needed feedback or when a parent had a question. In order for principals to support the implementation of the algebra curriculum as instructional leaders, a principal lab was essential.

Where are you in the adoption process?

No matter what, if you're supporting a teacher with new curriculum, you'll be supporting a teacher who's dealing with some level of insecurity. Depending on the timing of your lab, you may see different levels of insecurity manifest themselves in a variety of ways. If you're in the very early stages of curriculum adoption, for example, teachers may be more willing to admit vulnerability. There's a lot less perceived shame associated with being vulnerable if something is brand new. If your curriculum has been up and running for longer, though, you may need to lean into how to sustain your support when teachers are less likely to admit vulnerability. You probably recognize this in teachers who are afraid of being "found out" and so try to hide from support. Where you are in the adoption process should affect how you approach your feedback and support these teachers.

When we first began planning the lab to support our new algebra curriculum, we were initially nervous to reach out to the teachers involved. We wanted to bring in a room full of administrators in the first weeks of school when they were using a brand-new curriculum. It was a big ask, and we knew it. But, as it turned out, it wasn't as tough as we thought it might be. Once we explained to teachers that it would help their principals better support the learning they were doing, teachers were eager to get involved. Likewise, it's a big ask to invite principals to a full day of professional learning at the very beginning of the school year, but when we shared with them the vision for the day, many quickly responded that they were already getting questions from teachers and parents, and this would be just what they needed. Being purposeful to the timing of the lab and the adoption process was key to our success in this lab.

Relationship Building

How can you make your connector meaningful?

In a principal lab, much of the work that you do before the shared learning will serve as a connector. Whether you're offering coffee and greeting principals as they arrive to your building or you're touring a building to celebrate points of pride, you're building and strengthening important connections. We've found, though, that it's also important to plan for some strategic connectors depending on your group's needs and the type of lab. For example, once participants share their points of pride, you want to consider building on the conversation in ways that foster collaboration. In a lab to introduce new curriculum, a meaningful connector might involve engaging participants in an activity specific to the content or curriculum you'll be studying or by engaging in risk taking together to build trust.

When we planned our algebra lab, we'd already facilitated some math-specific principal labs in recent years, so we decided to focus on the theme rather than the content. One connector that we like for this purpose is the candy connector. This is just a simple way to engage participants in their own experiences related to the day's learning. To do this, offer a bowl of candy (anything multi-colored will work: Skittles, M&Ms, Jolly Ranchers, etc.), and ask participants to each take one (without sharing the question prompts). Then, based on the color, guide participants to find others who took the same color and reveal the question prompts so that participants can share their answers. Questions that we might assign to colors include the following:

- When was the last time you did something risky? How did you get through it?
- What's something about instruction that always makes you nervous?
- When was a time you learned to do something different from the way you've always done it? What was that process like for you?
- When has someone given you feedback that honored the risks you were taking? How did you know it honored your risk taking?

For this connector, we chose a reflective activity because we wanted to prompt participants to look inward. This personal reflection helped build the empathy and perspective taking that would be necessary to support teachers' risk taking throughout the lab.

What might you need to consider when grouping participants?

Whenever you're thinking of asking participants to work in small groups, you should consider whether you're going to intentionally assign them to their groups or let them choose for themselves. Letting participants choose their own groups can honor autonomy and strengthen existing relationships. We've found, though, that although it may often feel more comfortable to lean toward participant choice when it comes to grouping (this is probably true whenever facilitating among colleagues), we often decided to assign principals strategically into groups. When you do this, you'll want to ask yourself

- What strengths does each participant bring to the group?
- Who would benefit from working together?
- What experiences do they bring with them?

Our algebra lab brought together principals across both middle and high school buildings, and since principals often are curious about how the curriculum rollout is going for someone else, we tried to form observation groups that paired participants from across buildings and levels. We were also thoughtful to what each participant's experience was. For example, we had more than one principal who had previously taught in math classrooms. We made sure to split those participants up into different groups so that they could share their knowledge, experiences, and connections across multiple groups of participants.

Anchoring Experience

What is it you want your team to understand?

A principal doesn't need to know all the ins and outs of every curriculum resource in their building, but they do need to have a strong enough understanding to support its implementation. When you're preparing for a lab to introduce new curriculum, you want to make sure your participants will walk away with three key understandings.

1. Essential Elements of the Curriculum

To do this, plan together with curriculum consultants and/or teacher leaders to determine what those essential elements of this new curriculum might be. It might be helpful to think, "If the principals in my building could walk away understanding ___ about the new curriculum, the day would be a success." Once you've identified the essential elements of the curriculum that you want your participants to get familiar with, consider engaging principals in a demonstration lesson, reading an anchor article, or doing an analysis of the actual curriculum materials to suss out what the essential elements are that they'll be looking for.

Although a demonstration lesson could be a strong fit for labs to introduce new curriculum, we chose not to use it when we planned our lab to introduce the new algebra curriculum. We had already run several labs with demonstration lessons as anchoring experiences with elements similar to the algebra curriculum. For this lab, we knew that, since the curriculum was new and principals would be likely called upon to defend it to parents and stakeholders in addition to supporting their teachers through its adoption, it was more important to have participants deeply understand how this curriculum was supported by research and how it connected to other initiatives. We wanted to layer the new algebra curriculum into what was already established as the district vision, and studying an anchor article together allowed us to dig into a deepened level of understanding around this.

For our lab to study the new algebra curriculum, we asked principals and other participants to read an article that highlighted research on effective instruction that we knew was foundational in choosing this resource during the adoption process. Many teachers involved in the adoption process understood the "why," but we felt like, with as many things that were on principals' plates, fully understanding the "why" behind a new curriculum resource was often not a priority, so we found value in backing up to root ourselves in the research behind this choice. We read our selected article together through a lens of trying to suss out what we should be looking for when we see teachers implementing the new curriculum, then groups worked together to process their thinking and chart out their conclusions. This gave principals a shared understanding of what the curriculum "should" look like before they engaged with any classrooms that were beginning to implement it, and it helped them feel confident and equipped to have strong conversations about the pedagogy behind it.

2. Teacher and Leader Vulnerability

Lately in education, buzzwords like "grit" and "growth mindset" have unwittingly led educators and students to mistakenly believe if we just work a little harder, we'll overcome the challenges we're facing. This is problematic when applying the mindset to students and staff alike. In terms of student and professional learning, taking on the "grit" mentality of just putting in a little more work ignores the role that systems play in the teachers' and students' experience and can unfairly put the burden on them to find their own solutions to challenges instead of addressing the systemic issues that can contribute to or create a particular challenge. Implementing a new curriculum is, indeed, a challenge, but simply expecting teachers to work a little harder or put in a little more time would be a gross disservice to them and to the administrators who are serving as instructional leaders. As administrators engage in reflection that focuses on the inherent vulnerabilities associated with taking on new curriculum, this professional learning makes the profound shift away from *monitoring* to *mentoring* teachers' implementation.

To embrace this, we developed a protocol for reflection (Figure 4.2) that upends the "grit" mindset and instead acknowledges the vulnerability inherent in a risk-taking endeavor. We call it the GIVE reflection protocol because it acknowledges that teachers give of themselves to be vulnerable and take risks in their practice, and principals give of themselves to be vulnerable and engage as learners and offer support.

Following professional learning sessions or PLC discussions, we ask teachers to reflect on the four GIVE elements:

- Something I **grasp** in my new learning.
- **I'm** feeling nervous about. . . .
- The next **viable** step for me in enacting this learning is. . . .
- Please **extend** support that looks like ____ to help me be successful in this.

The *E* in our protocol is inspired by Brené Brown's (2018) work: "What might supporting it look like for you?" Addressing new curriculum and learning in this way helps make risk taking feel like less of an isolated act and instead reinforces learning as being a part of a community of support.

FIGURE 4.2

GIVE Reflection

G	I	V	E
Something I *grasp* in my new learning.	*I'm* feeling nervous about . . .	The next *viable* step for me in enacting this learning is . . .	Please *extend* support that looks like ____ to help me be successful in this.
Giving students roles can help them come to the conversation prepared and participate in meaningful ways.	*The noise level and managing the whole class.* *What if other groups are off task when I am listening to one group? What if they are on task but noisy? Will it look like I am letting my class be out of control?*	*I will try having students do a self-reflection of how they participated in their group discussions.*	*I would like to see how other classes are managing their group discussions. Are students participating (on and off task) similarly in my class and in others? Have other teachers figured out tips for managing groups that I could try?*

Ask teachers to use the reflection before the principal labs so that you can compile the results and bring them to participants. When principals can read through a compiled list of reasons their teachers felt nervous, it can be eye-opening and help identify patterns. In this way, it can shift the conversation away from "fixing" individual teachers and toward examining what systemic supports the principals in your lab could offer.

In our algebra lab, we brought principals the compiled reasons the teachers were feeling nervous with their new curriculum materials. As they read through the list, several principals were especially surprised to see that teachers were nervous their administrators wouldn't like hearing so much talking in the classroom. While they had originally thought their teachers knew that they understood the value of talk in the classroom, they realized that they might need to be more explicit in conveying this through their feedback. The GIVE reflection provided principal lab participants with an opportunity to hear from teachers in their building in a candid, safe way, and it was pivotal for framing the rest of the learning that would follow.

3. Priming for Feedback

Although the purpose of this lab is not to actually give the participating teachers immediate feedback on their observed lesson, part of the goal is increasing leaders' capacity to give feedback in the future. Because you know that after the observation, you'll work with participants to calibrate feedback, you'll want to think about how to get them ready to do that work beforehand. You'll be introducing participants to a model of the curriculum's intended implementation and then experiencing their teachers' own early stages of implementation, so it's important to think about how to frame the experience from an asset rather than a deficit approach so that all members of the team go in ready to think about feedback.

Whether through your observation template or through guiding questions you'd like them to focus on when in the classroom, prime your participants for the debrief that will follow by asking them to notice what risks they see teachers taking. This subtle shift in language will start guiding principals to take on the role of mentor while their teachers are experiencing Newkirk's "awkwardness principle."

Shared Observation

How do you choose and prepare host teachers for the observation?

This type of lab can offer critical professional learning opportunities for building and district administrators, but when you're talking about a new curriculum, it's fair to assume that all teachers involved are feeling that awkwardness principle to some degree, and the last thing you want to do is add another stressor to their plates. So, for us, this question was largely a matter of being in tune with teachers' confidence levels and ownership in professional learning. We also found that this depended on how early we were in the process of implementing the new curriculum. When we facilitated the lab to study a new algebra curriculum, it was within the first weeks of the school year and district-wide curriculum implementation. Throughout the year, we knew that all teachers implementing this curriculum would be supported heavily through a combination of in-district and external supports from the curriculum resource. Because we knew this support was coming, it was important for us to get a baseline understanding so that they could recognize and acknowledge teachers' achievements. Since we weren't looking for exemplar classrooms, we were looking to get a better sense of what taking on this curriculum looked like in its early stages, so we turned to multiple teachers who had received initial trainings and were taking on the associated learning. We didn't do much to prepare them other than to communicate our purpose and that we wanted them to teach whatever lesson they would have otherwise had that day however they were planning to teach it. In other words, it was important to us to see their implementation as authentically as possible and without interference. When we explained that this experience was designed to support their principals so that they could, in turn, better support them, teachers were far more comfortable sharing this vulnerability.

In another lab that we facilitated around a new science curriculum, the high school science teachers had been implementing for a few months, and we were just beginning a middle school rollout. Principals coming to the lab had a surface-level awareness of many of the new components of the curriculum, but they wanted to get a better understanding of what the curriculum looked like in action. For this reason, we wanted the shared observation to continue the anchoring experience and deepen the participants' understanding of what supported implementation should look like. In this case, we chose a host who had not only attended all professional learning, but who had also emerged as a leader in his department, volunteering for additional teacher learning labs and leading collaborative planning. Prior to the principal lab, he worked with the district's science coach to review his plans, and he looked forward to the coach's feedback following the principal lab.

It's hard to outline a set formula for choosing and preparing a host in a lab that has so much inherent vulnerability, but we've found that if we carefully consider how early we are in implementation, what our purpose is in the shared observation, and how each teacher might be feeling, we've been able to secure host teachers who have found the experience to be valuable even though it is the principals' learning that these labs are designed to support. Having the opportunity to observe their own teachers as hosts is critical for principals in this type of job-embedded professional learning lab because, instead of separating their learning from application, in-building hosts and observations help frame the concepts in the real-life happenings of the buildings where they work every day.

How should we structure our observations?

Because you want your participants to get a better sense of how to support their teachers, they should get a chance to better understand a wide range of what their teachers are experiencing, so it would be ideal to send them to the classrooms of multiple teachers. Likewise, you'd like them to see as much context surrounding what the teachers are experiencing as possible, so they should stay for a whole class period.

In our algebra lab, we split our participants into smaller mixed groups so that we could get perspectives from four different classrooms. We chose four teachers, some of whom had been piloting the new curriculum the previous year and some of whom had not. The groups included multiple perspectives, including principals, central office administrators, and consultants. Each group was assigned to a classroom, and we scheduled the observation so that every group would have the opportunity to see an entire class period from beginning to end.

During a classroom observation, it's important to allow participants to spend their cognitive energy on the observation itself without doing a lot of on-the-spot analysis, but it's also necessary to allow everyone an opportunity to collect their thoughts in a way that sets them up for the meaning making they'll do after the observation. So, for this lab, our observation form was simple, but its headings gently focused participants' observations on risk taking so that they would be ready to dig into this thinking in the debrief that would follow. See Figure 4.3 for an example of how we organized an observation form to do this.

FIGURE 4.3

Curriculum Observation Template

T = Teacher; S = Student; Ss = Students

Structure	Noticings (see/hear)	Connection to GIVE
Beginning	• Group roles taped to center of S tables. • T reviews warm-up, explains, "Today we're going to add to this by thinking about how. . . ." • T asks Ss to talk in groups to make plan for how to approach task. • T reminds Ss of group expectations, roles taped to tables.	In the "G" reflections, I noticed a lot of teachers were "grasping" establishing roles for group discussions. This teacher has evidence of trying that.
Middle	• S: "Wait, what are we supposed to do?" • T quickly circulates. Says, "Take out your book . . . page 23 . . . where is your pencil . . . ask your group." • S: "How do we want to figure this out?" • S: "In the warm-up, I tried. . . . Maybe if we do that first. . . ." • S taps another on arm: "Weren't you paying attention?" • One group puts books away. S announces, "We're done!" • S points at board: "Our first idea didn't work, so which should we try next?"	In the "I" reflection, many teachers said they were nervous about managing the class. Some students were off task, and some were using strategies collaboratively and self-monitoring staying on task. Teacher moved to a lot of tables—they must be tired!
End	• T calls on two students from clipboard to show their strategy and explain thinking. • Ss whisper to each other: "We didn't do it that way!" "You mean we did the whole thing wrong?" "No, I think ours is OK, too." • T displays Qs on screen: "How did your group do today? How do you know? What can you do tomorrow to make it better?" Some Ss talk about these Qs; some start packing up.	In the "V" reflection, some teachers mentioned a good next step might be having students self-reflect. T is trying this. How many students are participating? How might they increase ownership of this reflection?

Adapted with permission from Waterford School District.

Feedback and Feeding Forward

How can you structure discussion and debriefing to support your purpose?

Once participants have engaged in their observation to notice what the teacher is taking on, it's time to walk them through a debrief to build a deeper understanding of what they saw in the classroom and to support each other in giving feedback that is just right for that teacher.

We typically like to give each participant a few minutes of silent individual reflection to collect their thoughts on the connection side of the observation template immediately after the observation, and then after that, we recommend the following protocol to facilitate the discussion across groups of observers.

Step 1. Cross-pollinate Through Varied Grouping

Arrange participants into groups who didn't observe the same classrooms. Ask them to discuss the following prompt:

Before we traveled to our observations, we developed a vision of this curriculum's implementation. Discuss what actions you saw teachers taking on as part of this vision.

Having groups comprised of participants who observed different classrooms will give them an opportunity to gain a wider net of experiences. As they share their observations and draw connections, their conversation is likely to focus on identifying patterns rather than on defaulting to evaluation.

Step 2. Whole-Group Calibration

Bring everyone back together to begin thinking about prioritizing feedback. Together, revisit the GIVE responses from the teachers and make connections to what was observed in the classroom. In order to keep the conversation coming from an asset-based approach to support, you might consider asking questions like "What are they grasping well? What are they trying?"

At this point in the process, it's likely that participants are excited about a lot of what they saw. Some patterns may be naturally emerging in your discussion, but it's also easy to get sidetracked from supporting the curriculum implementation. To stay focused and to prepare for the next step of constructing feedback, it would be helpful to walk through one or both of the following activities:

Evaluation Calibration. If your school or district has a common evaluation tool or rubric, this is a good time to engage participants in a discussion about how it aligns with the curriculum vision and implementation. At this point, it is important to stress that the activity should *not* consist of rating the teachers you just observed. Rather, you might look through the rubric language to find parallels to your constructed vision, or you might identify areas where teachers are taking risks related to the GIVE reflection. Doing this can help administrators give feedback that is responsive and relevant.

Once principals in our lab returned from observing algebra classes in action, they unpacked what they saw through cross-pollinating discussion, but we needed the whole-group discussion to bring their learning to more concrete conclusions. The district uses the Charlotte Danielson rubric (Danielson, 2007) for teacher evaluation, so we asked participants to do a cross-walk between Domain 2 on the Danielson rubric and what they'd observed in their classroom—again, from an asset-based approach. We asked questions like

- Where are the risks that we saw teachers taking reflected on this rubric?
- What implications might this have as teachers continue to develop this learning?
- In what ways does this curriculum adoption support teachers' professional learning and growth?

Connecting our observations and conversations back to the rubric they use for evaluations helped principals think about how the pedagogy of the new curriculum aligns with the instructional vision they've developed for their district and school. This way, they could ensure their feedback would help connect the dots for teachers.

Big Rocks Prioritizing. Stephen Covey (2018) explains a good decision-making strategy for leaders by comparing priorities to rocks and gravel. The gist of it is that, if you have a vessel that you need to fill with rocks of varying sizes and you first fill it with all the tiny, gravel-sized rocks, it's unlikely you'll be able to fit the big rocks in on top, and you'll be left with a mess. But, if you first fill the vessel with the big rocks, the gravel will fill in the spaces between the big rocks, and you can make it all fit. Ask lab participants to determine what the "big rocks" are when it comes to implementing this new curriculum. Or, put another way, what are the most vital pieces to put into place first with the understanding that the rest can follow? You may choose to use an open-ended discussion or return to your evaluation tools to help determine these priorities.

For example, when principals were studying the new algebra curriculum, it was easy for conversations to get sidetracked by classroom management. It was only the second week of school, after all. Taking time to explicitly prioritize what we saw, though, helped participants understand that, in this case, most classroom management issues they observed were small rocks that could fall into place once the bigger rocks of engaging students in authentic tasks was underway.

Step 3. Return to Observation Groups to Construct Feedback

Participants then return to their original partners or small groups and provide another level of cross-pollination to hear from experiences in every classroom, have time to process, and be ready to apply their new thinking collaboratively. They'll see that their observation was not just an isolated experience, and they can begin to identify patterns as they work toward a rich understanding of their teachers' learning continuum.

Depending on the principals and administrators who are participating in your lab, it may be helpful to support this through some deeper learning into giving feedback. We've found that, oftentimes, when principals participate in professional learning about what their teachers are learning, they often feel some level of comfort in identifying when teachers are "doing it" or "aren't." The tricky part is responding in ways that will support the teachers rather than feel like a critique. When it came time for us to dig into this part of our algebra lab, we read an article on crafting quality feedback that is specific and actionable, and acknowledges the risks taken. Participants then returned to their groups to collaboratively craft feedback for the teacher they observed. Everyone then individually wrote a thank-you note to the teachers that highlighted one of the risks that they saw taken and implemented some of the feedback constructing advice from our shared article.

Whether you decide to share the feedback with the host teachers is up to you and your teams to decide. Your purpose is to practice crafting this feedback with your colleagues, so this is learning for you and your participants. It's likely that some of your teachers will want you to share that feedback, though. Regardless of what you decide, you should make sure to communicate very clearly with your teachers about what they can expect following the lab. They should know in no uncertain terms that the feedback you discuss will not be a part of their formal evaluation, but they should also know what you plan to share and how you plan to share it. For example, will you share feedback with every teacher host in written form, or through individual conferences? Or will they understand that they should reach out if they decide they'd like to get feedback on the observation?

The Heart of the Lab

In *Dare to Lead,* Brené Brown (2018) explains that the capacity to "rumble with vulnerability" is much easier said than done. In the case of new curriculum, teachers confront their vulnerability in implementing it, and principals navigate their own vulnerability around giving feedback in a content area that may already be outside their comfort zone.

To be sure, whenever there is new curriculum, there is bound to be a lot of "rumbling." When we first set out to study the new Algebra I curriculum, we were nervous about inviting administrators into classrooms so early in the school year, as there was bound to be a lot of "rumbling" from everyone involved. We were so glad that we did, though.

After the first round in the year's fall evaluation cycle, one building principal reached out to share that participating in the algebra lab had been critical when it came time to give teachers feedback. Having engaged in a lab to introduce new curriculum, she not only was able to better understand a new curriculum; she also felt better equipped to support her teachers. Investing in the opportunity to "rumble with vulnerability" and deepen our understanding of the risks related to a new curriculum was, indeed, well worth it.

FIGURE 5.1

Instruction Sample Agenda

Principal Lab Agenda
Instructional Best Practice

Morning

Relationship Building
- Points of Pride: Host Provides a Tour of the Building
- Team Building: Interesting Facts
- Strategy Implementation Guide

Anchoring Experience: NGSx Lesson Experience
Shared Observation
- Single Classroom Observation

Feedback and Feeding Forward
- Personal Reflection
  - Note Taking, Note Making
- Whole-Group Discussion
  - Revisit the Strategy Implementation Guide

Lunch

Afternoon

Learning Looks
- Visits
- Debrief

Feedback and Feeding Forward (Continued)
- Analyze, Group, Differentiate

Connections to Our Practice Reflection
- Feedback that Honors, Empowers, and Feeds Forward

Adapted with permission from Waterford School District.

5

Labs to Study
Instructional Practices

Regardless of your overall purpose and structure, every lab will in some way revolve around instruction. When you're working on supporting principals' roles as instructional leaders, that's just the nature of job-embedded professional learning labs. Labs to study instructional practices, though, are where the complexity and the interconnectedness of instruction throughout the building or district take center stage.

The primary purpose of these labs is to build principals' capacity to understand the best practices in their schools' classrooms so that they can collaboratively plan differentiated support for their instructional staff. See Figure 5.1 for a sample lab agenda for instructional best practices.

Administrators' strengths are diverse, and their backgrounds are even more varied. Some may have been in leadership positions for many years, and their classroom experience may, as a result, be distant or outdated. Others may have come from roles like counseling or physical education in which their experiences didn't closely resemble the instruction found in the majority of classroom teachers. Still others may have recently come from traditional instructional roles, but interests and strengths other than instructional leadership led them to their current leadership roles. Even when a team has considerable experience and expertise in the best practices you're studying, there is great power in building a common understanding and language around the vision you'll be supporting together.

In his article "Turning Around Schools: The Real Key to Success," Josh Martin (2019) explains the need for this focus:

> Simply having general knowledge—or conversational knowledge—of instruction isn't enough. A principal must know and understand instructional practices to a level that they are comfortably able to put those practices in place to address diagnosed instructional weaknesses. While it is naive to think principals can be experts in every content area on their campuses, it should be expected that principals know and are capable of sharing quality instructional strategies and practices that transcend content areas.

Supporting principals in developing this instructional expertise along with a collaborative network for ongoing support will, in turn, develop participants' individual and collective efficacy as instructional leaders.

We have turned to this type of lab time and time again over the past several years. Though the focus may shift a bit and the specific facilitation moves we use throughout the lab change for each one, we've found that starting with some key questions helps us prepare a lab to study instructional practices that is meaningful for all participants.

Determining Focus

What do you value in instruction?

This is the first and quite possibly the most important question. Ultimately, you need to work together to determine how to articulate the experiences every student deserves as a part of your school, district, or institution. It may be tempting to rush through it in order to get down to logistics, but we'd strongly caution you not to shortchange this question. The discussions you'll have around your values will lay the groundwork for everything that follows. This is a question you'll discuss with your cofacilitators as you plan for the lab and with all of the participants once you're participating in the labs themselves. Because this question speaks directly to the organization's vision, it should be a starting place for every continuous improvement goal and every professional learning initiative. It must be clearly understood, articulated, and shared among all stakeholders. This is particularly important for principals as instructional leaders, as they are the stakeholders who so often drive the culture of instruction in their building through their feedback and the professional learning they plan for their staff.

Have you ever heard from staff that they felt like they were constantly experiencing professional learning whiplash from being yanked back and forth between the latest speakers and initiatives? You might hear these teachers say things like "Just wait it out. This'll go away by next year, and then we'll learn the next big thing we're supposed to be doing." When this happens, it's usually because professional learning isn't centered around a clearly articulated vision or set of values.

As a principal, rather than pivot to each new initiative that presents itself, you can commit to staying the course with the values you collaboratively identify. When all members of your instructional leadership team can share with staff a common message about instructional values that are woven throughout "the fabric of your organization" (Harhsak, Aguirre, & Brown, 2010), you're much more likely to stay focused and avoid this whiplash phenomenon.

We've worked with districts that start values and visioning work before beginning any principal labs, but in other cases, these conversations have come up throughout the process of planning and facilitating principal labs. They may emerge from a book study, a deep dive into research, classroom observations, or even hallway conversations. No matter how this work bubbles up, we've found that it's crucial to bring it out and develop it intentionally. When you're an instructional leader, there's no wrong time to ask questions like the following:

- How does research shape my vision of what instruction looks like?
- How does my vision align with other leaders' visions in my building?
- How does it align across buildings in my district?
- How does what I see happening in classrooms in my building align to this vision?
- What steps might I need to take to better build a collective vision?

What are the high-yield practices that will help you get there?

Once you're clear on your group's shared values, you understand where you're coming from, or your "why." Next, you need to explore where you're going, or the "what" in terms of instruction. To do this, you'll want to dig into a deeper understanding of the essential elements of instruction that are present throughout the content areas and levels that you support.

It's easy—too easy—to compartmentalize instruction. We think in terms of our individual curriculum or grade levels. We separate by grade level or subject area for PLC, PD time, and planning. And in doing so we create silos: areas of content that are disconnected from one another when they should be connected by the common threads of instruction. For a building principal, navigating silos can lead to the frustrating feeling that you need to be an expert in everything, but then you realize that it's ultimately impossible.

Instead, understanding common threads that run throughout content areas can help principals to see beyond the silos and better support many content areas. Rather than feeling like you have to fully shift with each content classroom you visit, recognizing common instructional elements can make your feedback and support less disconnected and daunting. In order to help your participants understand common instructional threads that run through existing silos, you'll need to anchor the lab in a shared experience. Much like labs to introduce new curriculum, you need to build capacity in what you're striving for so the practices can be deeply implemented.

While we were working with one district, many departments were working on separate content-specific professional learning initiatives. Science teachers were learning about the newly adopted NGSS standards, language arts teachers were expanding literature circles and book clubs in their secondary classrooms, and middle school math teachers were navigating a relatively new curriculum resource. It would be easy for a building principal to feel like they had a lot of new initiatives to learn and support, so we knew it was important to help them make connections between them.

The district had already outlined a focus on the gradual release of responsibility as a key component in their instructional vision, and the collaboration within that was a common thread tying all of these content-specific initiatives together. It was a value that was critical when the district determined "the fabric of their organization" (Harhsak et al., 2010), but it was also one that our own formative assessment through observations and surveys showed needed support across the board. So, we set out to plan a series of labs—both instructional labs for teachers and principal labs—to study collaboration in instruction.

What does success look like within these practices?

In labs that introduce new curriculum, you examined the role of administrators in supporting risk taking. Again, this is a critical component of studying instructional practices. Rather than identifying teachers who simply "have it" or don't, you'll work to identify indicators along a continuum so that you can systematically support teachers as they grow in their practice.

Many, Maffoni, Sparks, and Thomas (2018) describe a tool that they call a Strategy Implementation Guide (SIG): "The SIG is a developmental tool that supports teacher teams, coaches, and school leaders in articulating a team's current reality, identifying implementation gaps and designing next steps" (p. 51). This document gives everyone involved, from teachers to principals to central office administrators, a guide for common language and understanding. This framework helped us establish our own document that we call an Instructional Continuum Guide (ICG). In changing the name, we broadened the context from a single strategy to instructional practice, and we wanted to emphasize that educators are learners on a continuum rather than operating within checkboxes where they either have it or don't. At the end of the continuum, we identify the long-term goals of the instructional change. In other words, if teachers move along the continuum to full implementation, then the result will be _____. This helped us define shorter actionable steps that are attached to loftier long-term goals. We also worked to adapt the tool to fully utilize appreciative inquiry. We recognize that even the smallest moves from teachers, when acknowledged and supported, can lead to large changes in instruction. Because of this, we use the initial indicator column to acknowledge some of the small teacher actions that it takes before any changes in student actions occur.

We use this guide not as an evaluative tool but as one for responsive formative assessment so that administrators can give stronger support between evaluations and so that teachers know and have a say in what their evaluators are looking for. Because of this, we found that in order for the tool to be effective, the same principles of responsive formative assessment apply.

First, this guidance document should be developed with the learners around the shared learning. In order to do this, you'll want to build the success indicators collaboratively. It may seem like it would be more efficient to present participants with a premade rubric or checklist, but investing in the process to build a resource like this together is invaluable. It will serve as a vehicle to build your common understanding and language together, and it will help your participants develop ownership in the work.

To do this, you'll want to introduce a template to collect indicators for success at increasing levels of implementation. See Figure 5.2 for how we adapted a SIG by Many et al. (2018) for principal labs, or go to the appendix to find a blank version. On it, we decide what indicators look like in at least three categories representing a continuum of implementation. Our goal was to work toward a shared understanding of where teachers were on the continuum, so the discussions to craft language that describes our observations and other formative data as indicators of success were perhaps just as important—if not more so—than the actual language of the indicators that we settled on.

When you're working together to determine the language to describe the instructional moves that go in each of these categories, we found that we tended to frame our language either on consistency (e.g., sometimes, always) or on success (e.g., effectively, strategically), depending on the instructional component that is described. In Figure 5.2, we've compiled and adapted language that we developed with principals in a lab where we studied collaboration in instruction in content areas. In the "Initial Indicators" column, we worked to name small steps that principals might notice when they enter the room of a teacher who is just beginning implementation. For example, we noted in this column that principals might expect to see these teachers move around the room rather than sitting at their own desk. In the next column, we stated that teachers who are moving beyond these initial phases to partial implementation might sometimes circulate through the room for formative assessment. Once teachers take on full implementation of the strategy, we note in the third column that principals might expect to see that these teachers frequently and strategically circulate throughout the room to check for understanding. Recognizing this throughline in concrete steps can help principals give more specific feedback, and it can help them recognize even the earliest indicators of implementation so that they can celebrate risk taking and work from an asset-based mindset.

FIGURE 5.2

Collaborative Learning ICG

	Initial Indicators	Partial Implementation	Full Implementation
	What will you see or hear that supports first steps in implementation?	What will you see or hear to show ongoing attempts at implementation?	When will you know that the indicator has become a part of daily practice?

Collaborative Learning	• Teacher language and actions support
	  ○ Risk taking
	  ○ Respect
	  ○ Support
	• Complexity of task includes
	  ○ Sharing not solving
	  ○ Parallel work
	• Groups are attempted
	• Language:
	  ○ Teacher uses academic language
	  ○ Teacher prompts for use of language
	• Teacher moves throughout the room.
		• Teacher and student language or actions include some
		  ○ Risk taking
		  ○ Respect
		  ○ Support
		• Complexity of task may include
		  ○ Processing
		• Grouping is appropriate to task or student needs
		• Individual or group accountability
		• Language:
		  ○ Some academic language used
		  ○ Some scaffolding for language skills
		• Teacher sometimes circulates to formatively assess and provide guided instruction
			• Teacher and student language and actions consistently include
			  ○ Risk taking
			  ○ Respect
			  ○ Support
			• Complexity of task may include
			  ○ Resolving problems
			  ○ Reaching consensus
			  ○ Identifying solutions
			• Intentional grouping is
			  ○ Appropriate to task
			  ○ Appropriate to students' needs
			• Individual and group accountability
			• Language:
			  ○ Academic language used consistently
			  ○ Appropriate scaffolding for language skills
			• Teacher strategically circulates to formatively assess and provide guided instruction

Full implementation of this component over time will result in

• Increased student engagement
• Improved understanding and test scores

Staffwide and individual teacher celebrations:

Second, it's important to enter into this work with the understanding that your ICG is not a static document. It may change and shift over time as the learning shifts. Because of this, we found that it was critical to circle back on this language repeatedly as the year progressed to check our understanding and see if our original wording and indicators were still appropriate or might need tweaking. Yes, you'll put a lot of time into the document in the first place, but don't let that keep you from opening it up for revision. Ongoing discussions around revision will only serve to continue to deepen shared understanding of the instruction you're studying.

As we were establishing our ICG, we wanted to deepen our understanding of how it might function within systems and structures that were already in place. To do this, we examined how elements that we had established as "full implementation" aligned with the evaluation rubric the district used. It was important to us that labs never ran the risk of taking on the purpose of evaluating or rating, so we did these cross-walks with general indicators on the ICG and wholly separate from discussion about specific observations.

Anything that takes on the appearance of a rubric runs the risk of feeling evaluative, and we were duly concerned about that. Through collaborative development of the document, returning to it often, and treating it as a live tool to collect our learning, we found that the ICG moved out of the realm of evaluation. This tool proved to be essential to help principals give formative feedback and make plans for differentiation. For example, a building administrator in a middle school started to use the tool to differentiate how she gave feedback following informal observations. If she noticed multiple teachers working on the complexity of the collaborative tasks they designed, she debriefed with them together, and when she noticed teachers working in the full implementation indicator in particular areas, she invited others in to observe their classes. Following one of our labs to study instructional practices, an assistant principal from another building shared with us that he used the ICG individually with teachers during meetings following formal observations, but where he used the district's evaluation rubric to assign scores, he used the ICG to give feedback that was actionable and to better help the teachers understand the reasoning behind each score. Because it was a document that was created collaboratively and within the context of his own district, it felt more like a living, influential tool than one that was premade or developed by an author outside the organization. After using it to support teachers on a continuum, this assistant principal reported that his follow-up conversations resulted in better reflection and made the evaluation process feel more purposeful.

Upon the conclusion of a series of labs to develop and craft feedback based on an ICG, one building principal summed up why the process and the tool were valuable. He explained that the ICG "gives all of us, teachers and administrators, a set of common talking points and benchmarks for the critical components of our practice. Additionally, its development has been a collaborative process between teachers, curriculum development staff, and administration. By working together to both identify and define the standards, there is a much greater level of understanding for all of us as to what it actually 'looks like' when a component is fully implemented."

Relationship Building

Who needs to participate?

Much like with labs to introduce new curriculum, you want all stakeholders, from building to central office, to achieve vertical alignment in your support.

You certainly may decide to focus on a particular level or building at a time, but labs to study instructional practices also offer the opportunity for more creative and flexible grouping. This is where it might be particularly advantageous to cross between levels and have secondary and elementary principals visit each other's classrooms to study instructional practices K–12.

When we devoted a year to studying collaboration, principal labs early in the year kept middle and high school administrators together, but we quickly found that they were curious how they could build off collaborative instruction happening in the elementary buildings, so for a later lab in our series, we brought K–12 principals together to study what it meant to collaborate throughout the district.

Labs to study instructional practices also offer the opportunity to build common language with all those involved in the instructional values you're studying. For example, in an elementary lab studying the implications of social-emotional learning in core instruction, we knew that it was critical to bring social workers in as participants in the lab. In the district, social workers were often split between buildings, so they provided a natural connection and path toward coherence. But, with caseloads that keep their days packed, we recognized that they were often not a part of professional learning around instruction even though their voices were likely some of the most important ones at the table when it came to social emotional learning.

Principal labs have the potential to move beyond the diagnostic space of instructional rounds largely because of their collaborative nature toward learning. Being thoughtful to who's in the room is a key step in crafting this deeper learning experience.

What connectors might serve your purpose best?

Any type of connector can work for a lab to study instructional practices because, by their nature, these labs encompass a wide range of topics and contents. When you're planning how to get principals to connect with each other and to the day's topic, the most important thing is to ask yourselves what this group needs in order to set the tone for the day and get the group working together. In labs that study instructional practices, it can be easy to focus entirely on the teachers and the instruction happening in their classrooms, but the real value in the principal labs comes in having principals connect their understanding of the topic to their own practice as instructional leaders.

In some cases, you might choose a connector that is tied to or reflective of the instructional practice you're studying so that principals can begin re-engaging in the instructional practice if they haven't otherwise been focused on it. If, for example, you're digging into collaborative learning or discourse, you might choose a connector that brings out communication skills. Oftentimes, from a building principal's perspective, a new instructional initiative can feel like another thing on a to-do list, so having an opportunity to experience and reflect on an aspect of the instruction as an active participant can be a helpful way to ground principals in an instructional focus.

Because we've found that these labs can be one of the most common labs to run, though, you might also find that you're more focused on team building than on the lab's instructional focus. Principal labs require participants to learn together in a collaborative environment, and this is not always something that is already in place when administrators typically see each other for regular district-level meetings. Whenever you're bringing together principals with different backgrounds or from multiple buildings, they likely need some team building if they are going to collaborate together as learners. Sometimes they come together from competing buildings and you're working to help them see each other as resources, not rivals. Other times, there may be power dynamics in play if you have multiple levels of building administrators, such as principals, assistant principals, and deans. We've found that it's important to be attuned to the social-emotional needs of principals as participants in designing connected activities that will build a collaborative culture. As we were working to establish our collaborative relationships, we used icebreakers and team-building activities as connectors in many of these labs. Because we know that these kinds of connectors can sometimes feel disjointed, we've found that it's important in facilitation to explain to the group why we chose that particular connector and how we're hoping it serves the group's needs.

For example, in one lab where participants were just getting to know one another across their buildings and roles, we had each participant submit two to three little-known facts about themselves to the facilitator before the lab. As a connector, then, we presented all of these facts in a list and instructed the participants to interview each other in order to determine who each fact belonged to, but we made the interviews a little trickier with the following stipulations:

- They could only ask two questions to each person.
- They may not use any of the words in the fact itself in their questioning.

The facts that they shared were goofy and ranged from golf awards to getting lost on vacation, and the interviews were fun because everyone was challenged by trying to stay within the parameters of the game's rules. After a set time for interviews, we shared the real answers, learned that some of us had things in common that we never would have known otherwise, and then we reflected on the process. Principals, curriculum consultants, and central office administrators shared that they had fun getting to know one another better and that they all felt like the rules put them on equally challenging footing.

Anchoring Experience

How should you structure the lab space?

Regardless of the space available to you, it's important to make every effort to configure the space in ways that will best fit the needs of each portion of your lab. The setup of the room during the anchoring experience should mimic the instruction you'll be studying in classrooms. If you're digging into collaborative instruction, move desks or tables into small groups. Or, if you're introducing the concept of restorative practices, it might make sense to start the whole group sitting in a circle.

Be ready to shift, then, for the varying needs of the lab components. Your observation analysis might need participants to form new groups. This can be tricky in any environment, but especially so in one that may have limited space. Think creatively about all available spaces. In the absence of tables or wall space, you might move into the hallway and anchor your poster or sticky notes to lockers. In the end, the most important thing about your space is not that it's beautifully designed or ultra-contemporary; it's that it can support your overall purposes for analysis and collaboration.

How can you create a shared understanding of the instruction you're studying?

Articles and research always offer an opportunity to create some shared learning, but we've found that, when we're studying instruction, participants actually experiencing the instruction is one of the most powerful anchoring experiences we can offer.

When a school's science department was taking on new units aligned to the NGSS science standards, which required the paradigm shift from learning about science to figuring out science, district administrators needed to understand the shift teachers were making. To do this, we worked with the district's K–12 science consultant to develop an anchoring experience that would help principals experience this shift. As one of the first things on the agenda following connecting activities, he took on the role of teacher while the principals and other participants in the lab became the students. He showed a video of a tanker train car that imploded seemingly out of nowhere and then explained that we'd develop an initial model to try to explain why. He then moved the participants into groups to make their predictions. Once the groups made their predictions, they used two-liter bottles, water, and chart paper to bring that real-world phenomenon to their tabletop.

After experiencing phenomena-forward instruction firsthand, the consultant stepped out of his science teacher role and into a facilitating role within the lab to discuss with the principals what elements of the lesson they might expect to see in classrooms throughout their buildings. Although experiencing the lesson itself was valuable, this debrief was crucial because it helped principals reflect on their experience and to move forward with a common understanding so that they could be more responsive to supporting teachers with feedback that took into account their phenomena-forward instructional shift.

Shared Observation

Which classrooms do you want to visit?

In labs that study instructional practices, you want to get a better pulse on the instruction happening throughout your building or your district so that you can strategically plan how to support teachers as they move forward. In this work, it's important to build the understanding not only of the practices themselves, but also that the process of developing best practices is one that is a trajectory rather than a binary system. That is, you want to avoid creating the mentality of identifying teachers who "either have it or they don't." Instead, you want to examine and better understand the depth of how practices are implemented in classrooms as teachers take on the learning.

If you choose to bring participants together to one full-class observation, it's important to position the host teacher as a teacher along a continuum and a leader rather than an exemplar or a case study in need of intervention. See Figure 5.3 for an example of an observation template that we've used in the past for lab participants to note observations in a table format. Two rows separate teachers and students, and each column focuses on what the participants see and hear and then how that behavior connects to the ICG. We've found that, before moving into the observation portion of the agenda, it's a helpful transition to tell the story of how and why we chose the host. We might explain leadership qualities that we've noticed throughout their professional learning, or we might explain what professional learning they've engaged in. If we've supported them in planning for the lab, we're up front about it. We want to take the magic out of instruction so that we can really start to analyze how to support it.

FIGURE 5.3

Instruction Observation Template

	Noticings (see/hear)	Connection to ICG
Teacher	• "Turn and talk in your groups about how you got this answer." • Teacher walks around the room, listening to groups. Stops periodically to add to conversations and answer questions. • "That was a good idea." • "What else could you try?" • "I'm glad you shared that."	• Processing (partial?) • Formatively assessing as they circulate—partial • Teacher is encouraging, respectful throughout interactions—full
Student	• Students get out cards that have conversation stems on them. Some ignore; some look at and use stems on the cards during conversation. ○ "I agree with . . . because . . ." ○ "Another way of thinking about that is . . ." • Two groups finish conversations quickly: "We're done." • "I got this. What did you get?"	• Some scaffolding provided; some groups may need additional support—partial • Some students are sharing, not solving during task—initial

While working with a language arts department that had been engaged in professional learning about moving away from teaching a whole-class novel and toward integrating more student choice in reading, the teachers were nervous that their administrators wouldn't understand what they were seeing because it looked so different from how classes had been structured in the past. This was the perfect opportunity for a lab to study instructional practice. After an anchoring experience that asked participants to examine how their own experiences in language arts compared to a model lesson facilitated by the district's language arts consultant, all lab participants traveled to the same middle school language arts classroom. We selected the classroom because, in addition to attending professional learning with the whole department, the teacher had taken on additional leadership and learning opportunities as she participated in teacher learning labs and volunteered for curriculum review committees. Throughout her participation, she had enough trust in her colleagues to share what aspects of the new learning made her nervous, and she was open to sharing her reflections. In this case, this teacher's leadership made her a good candidate to be a host teacher because she was clearly invested in the instructional practice, had relatively high efficacy, and was open to reflecting on and sharing her learning with others.

Because having all of the district's administrators watch your lesson at the same time can feel like a high-pressure situation, we asked her what kind of support would help her feel most comfortable. She opted to teach a lesson that she had coplanned with her colleagues during their PLC, and she asked for one-on-one coaching around implementing the plans before and after her lesson. It was important that she taught a lesson she had planned herself, and coaching helped her reflect on the decisions she'd made so that she could more confidently own them going into the lab.

We brought all participants to observe the same lesson because, in this particular lab, it was important we continued to calibrate around the instructional practice. In this way, the shared observation acted as a kind of extension of the anchoring experience. Lab participants got to see the instructional moves in a real context and outside the vacuum of a model lesson so they could get a better idea of what they could expect to see in daily interactions.

As long as participants are well-grounded in the instruction you're studying through the anchoring experience, it isn't always necessary to have all participants engage in a shared observation together. In fact, we've found that labs that study instructional practices are often most effective when participants get the opportunity to see multiple classrooms across varied content areas and depths of implementation. Therefore, a key component of labs to study instructional practices is the opportunity to participate in learning looks. As mentioned in Chapter 2, learning looks are short dips into multiple classrooms as opposed to more in-depth observations that take place over the course of the entire lesson. In order to bring a wide range of experiences into the conversation, you'll want to split your participants into smaller groups for learning looks observations.

Learning looks can be used on their own, or you can use them in conjunction with a larger shared observation. For many of our labs to study instructional practices, we planned for both. In our lab to study instruction in middle school language arts, we all traveled to the same classroom to observe a whole lesson; then after reflection and some analysis, we then split into smaller groups for learning looks to cast a wider net of what the instructional practices might look like across many classrooms. We gave participants a list of language arts teachers and their room numbers who had classes during that particular time, and each group traveled to two or more classes. While they didn't observe a whole class period, they dipped into each for at least 10–15 minutes to look for evidence of student choice and to observe different ways each teacher was implementing professional learning to integrate more student choice. While lab participants used the whole-group shared observation to deepen their understanding of the instructional practice, these learning looks offered the opportunity to gather more data to better understand the many ways the instructional practice might look in action. This would help us begin to identify varying levels of implementation. See Figure 5.4 for an example of one way that we have organized observation notes during learning looks. We created a table to write notes and observations, with each classroom down the rows and a column each for student and teacher behaviors.

When you're planning for learning looks, you don't want your principals to feel like they're wandering aimlessly or your teachers to feel like they're ambushed, so it's important to plan ahead how participants might know which classrooms to visit. For one of our labs to study collaboration in instruction, we relied on teachers inviting the lab participants into their classrooms themselves. In another, we were studying the first and last 10 minutes of secondary teaching periods, so we had to organize the schedule ahead of time to ensure principals would be in classrooms at the right time to see these portions of the lessons. See Figure 5.5 for an example of how this schedule looked divided by the first and last 10 minutes of each hour.

Not too long ago, a trend took hold among educators thanks to social media. In an effort to open themselves up to feedback from their peers, teachers posted signs outside their doors that invited others to #observeme (Kaplinsky, 2016). To replicate this spirit of ownership over the experience and extend it into getting administrators into classrooms, we explained to teachers the purpose of the learning happening in the principal labs, announced the times we'd be observing, and provided half-sheets with our own hashtag invitation. During our year-long series on collaboration in the Waterford School District, we used the hashtag

FIGURE 5.4

Learning Looks Observation Template

	Student Behaviors (see/hear)	Teacher Behaviors (see/hear)
LA8 Room #102	End of class period Students have notebooks, colored pens, and checklists on desks. • "What do you think was the most convincing evidence in this paragraph?"	• Announces: "We have five minutes left. Take a look at your checklist. If there are any questions you haven't asked your group yet, please do that now." • "On your exit ticket, please write to me your plan for one revision you might make to your essay based on your peer conferences today."
LA6 Room #114	Beginning of class period Chapter 2 comprehension questions on board. ○ Some students answer questions in notebook, some read, some talk. ○ "What did you put?"	• Takes attendance. • Circulates through rows, checking notebooks. Asks student in gray shirt, "Did you read the chapter last night?" • "As you finish, turn and talk to check your answers."
LA6 Room #127	Middle of class period • Sitting at tables with books. Each table has a different book that they are discussing. • "What part of this chapter should we start with?" • "What did you think it meant when the character said . . . ?"	• Moves to back left table, listens, and prompts student in gray shirt. • "If you get stuck, don't forget about your sticky notes."

#WSDcollaborates. Teachers who wanted to invite others in posted this sign outside their classroom door. We then told principals that, during learning looks, they could visit any classroom that had the sign. This gave our administrators quick visual clues to know which rooms to visit so that they could more comfortably engage in these informal observations.

How do you invite lab participants to engage within the observation?

When we first started facilitating principal labs to study collaborative instructional practices, we used a basic template for observations where participants simply documented what they saw and heard. Throughout our series of labs to study this instructional practice, we adjusted the observation protocol to be able to focus the observers' attention in different ways. Sometimes they alternated between focusing on student observations and the teachers' moves. Once participants were familiar

FIGURE 5.5

Learning Looks Structured Schedule

3rd Hour First 10 Minutes 9:45–9:55

Name	Subject	Room #
Teacher	Math 6	101
Teacher	Math 7	100
Teacher	LA 6	112
Teacher	Math 6	103
Teacher	LA 6	106
Teacher	SS 8	211

3rd Hour Last 10 Minutes 10:20–10:30

Name	Subject	Room #
Teacher	SS 6	111
Teacher	Sci 6	5
Teacher	Sci 7	2
Teacher	SS 7	6
Teacher	Reading 7	110
Teacher	SS 7	112

4th Hour First 10 Minutes 10:35–10:45

Name	Subject	Room #
Teacher	Sci 7	2
Teacher	ESOL	106
Teacher	LA8	208
Teacher	SS 8	212
Teacher	Algebra I	213
Teacher	Math 8	206

4th Hour Last 10 Minutes 11:02–11:12

Name	Subject	Room #
Teacher	Sci 6	105
Teacher	LA 6	110

4th Hour Last 10 Minutes 11:10–11:20

Name	Subject	Room #
Teacher	Gym	Gym
Teacher	Art 6	304

with the ICG, we put that at the top of the observation page and offered an opportunity for open note taking underneath it. In this way, participants could focus their observations on how the tool they'd developed aligned with what they saw and heard in the classroom.

Feedback and Feeding Forward

How can you structure discussion and debriefing to support your purpose?

The ultimate goal of this lab component is to help participants differentiate support for teachers in their building. Differentiation in education is widely regarded as something educators do for students, but we contend that the need for differentiation extends beyond just students and to all learners, which includes teachers and administrators. Tomlinson (2017) explains, "In a differentiated classroom, the teacher assumes that different learners have differing needs and proactively plans lessons that provide a variety of ways to 'get at' and express learning." The goal of instructional leaders, then, is to provide similar proactive planning for supporting teachers' differing needs. Just as this concept of differentiation is complex for teachers in planning for students, it is complex when planning to support educators. There is no one magic tip or tool to help educators better differentiate for a variety of needs; rather, it is important to build a deep understanding not only of the concept but also of the variety of needs that learners encounter within that concept. To help participants build that deep understanding, we have used a variety of structured discussions to help process the day's experience and move it forward into actionable learning.

Cocreating Success Indicators

If your participants have not yet cocreated a tool like our ICG, using their observation data to collaborate and determine a shared understanding of success indicators can be a helpful step in grounding the group and their learning. To do this, we have looked together at observation notes and lesson plans to parse out what it meant for collaboration to fall into the category of the ICG that reflected the fullest level of implementation.

Evidence on a Continuum

For this activity, we asked participants to go through their observation notes. We asked them to take individual observations of what they saw and heard and put each on an individual sticky note without any indicator of which classroom or which observer they came from. Then, we invited participants to place each sticky note along a shared space (a wall, a whiteboard, or a row of lockers all work well for this space) in a continuum of evidence.

As each participant shared a sticky note with an observation, they said, "I saw . . . ," or "I heard . . . ," as they experienced each observation without judgment. Then, we asked the group where that particular piece of evidence fell according to the ICG tool they had developed. Once the group reached consensus, the participant who made the observation placed that sticky note on the horizontal continuum. Just as English teachers engage in norming around a rubric or grading an essay, this activity was helpful in building a shared, or normed, way to interpret what administrators see and hear in their observations so that they can give more consistent feedback.

Analyze, Group, Differentiate

This protocol invites lab participants to look at observation data, much like in the evidence on a continuum activity, in terms of a range of implementation, and it prompts participants to plan for responding to that range. To facilitate this activity, invite participants to sort observation notes along the range of the ICG implementation indicators. You may do this by having them sort sticky notes into the ICG categories on a chart or by using three different markers to color-code findings on the observation note-taker according to the three ICG categories. Doing this visually helps participants to quickly range-find and see patterns that run throughout their classrooms and teachers.

Once the group has done this range-finding and sorting, we prompt participants to begin thinking about how they might use their findings to differentiate support. We do this by asking questions like the following:

- What does this tell us about the teachers in our building?
- What does this tell us about our learning plan so far?
- How can we strategically support groups of teachers?
- Which learning might be best for a whole group?
- Which learning goals might best be suited for smaller group or individualized feedback?

We then asked participants to work collaboratively in small teams to reflect on the teachers they were each responsible for supporting and evaluating so that they could begin planning supports for specific groups of teachers. By having principals work together to plan for groups of specific teachers, these instructional leaders were able to think about how they might systematize and differentiate their supports.

The Heart of the Lab

When a principal takes on the role of an instructional leader, it's easy to get overwhelmed by the sheer breadth of content in any one building. Labs to study instructional practices help participants build efficacy to give feedback in content areas and instructional practices in which they may not initially have background or expertise through differentiation. The depth of this work is great, and Carol Ann Tomlinson (2017) explains, "In a differentiated classroom, teaching is evolutionary." So, too, is instructional leadership. Rather than "train" in a particular area for a static understanding, principals who engage in this work will develop a deeper understanding of how to evolve and differentiate support for their teachers regardless of content area.

In these labs, participants collaborate within a shared vision to develop common understanding and a continuum of implementation as they study the instruction that makes up the "fabric of the organization" (Harhsak et al., 2010). This gives you the opportunity to study instruction vertically, to bring high school principals into elementary classrooms and vice versa. And it invites participants to look at commonalities between science lessons and the latest initiatives in reading instruction. As you're facilitating labs to study these instructional practices that tie the fabric together, you'll know the labs are paying off when principals see beyond content-area silos, make connections, and differentiate support for their teachers.

FIGURE 6.1

Network Sample Agenda

Principal Learning Agenda
Growing the Network

Morning

Relationship Building
- Building Points of Pride and Introductions
- The Power of Perspective: Drawing Connecter

Anchoring Experience
- Article Reading
  - Pair Prompt: Insights and Ah-ha's
  - Square Prompt: What patterns or themes emerged?

- Self-Assessment
  - Personal Reflection
  - Partnership Reflection

Shared Observation: Learning looks
- Pair Buildings for Visits: Lens of Celebrating Evidence

Lunch

Afternoon

Feedback and Feeding Forward
- Debrief
- Observation Sort
- Collaborative Planning

Reflect
- Whole-Group Conversation: What's lingering with you?
- Formative Assessment: How do we monitor and celebrate small wins?
- Final Reflection: Name a "small win" that you can celebrate tomorrow with your staff.

Adapted with permission from Waterford School District.

6

Labs to Build a
Network of Leaders

One of the most daunting feelings as a leader is the sense that you are doing the work alone. And it's easy for a principal to feel alone. It can feel like the weight of the school rests on your shoulders. From everyday policy to test scores, the principal is often the one who bears the brunt of the responsibility—at least in the public's eyes. Because of this, it's easy for those in administrative positions to feel as though they need to tackle it all on their own as a hero or martyr. But, taking on the weight of change yourself is not only tiring—it isn't terribly effective. Principals who establish a network of leaders within their building dramatically increase the likelihood of the instructional change they're striving for. Isabel Sawyer and Marisa Ramirez Stukey (2019) explain, "Administrators, along with teachers, must delve into the work together wondering, investigating, and seeking solutions to complex problems. The notion of leaders as 'heroes' must be dispelled and replaced with a collaborative approach" (p. 41). A savvy principal will recognize the value in this collaborative approach: that many perspectives and roles—from teachers to counselors to ancillary staff—are necessary when building a system for supporting instructional change.

Although all labs work to build this network by developing principals' perspectives and collaborating with participants, labs that build a network of leaders are designed to provide building leaders an opportunity to invite those who are an influential part of their system yet who may not typically attend principal labs, to create a network for collaborative learning around systemic support for change. In these labs, the focus shifts slightly away from the principals' own learning and toward sharing in that learning with others. Through this network, participants will expand their perspectives to work toward a more systemic approach, and they will leverage the lab opportunity as they plan to bring their learning back to their buildings with the newfound support of an expanded network of leaders for more hands on deck in their collaborative team.

Determining Focus

If you're thinking about planning a lab to build a network of leaders (see a sample agenda in Figure 6.1), it's easy to jump to the question of *who* you want to join your team. After all, you'll nearly double your attendance as each principal will invite a leader to attend alongside them. But we've found that it isn't the only question involved in planning. Before you get ready to invite leaders to your lab, we recommend thinking of some additional questions that will help you determine the focus and make your lab more meaningful: *why, what, who,* and *how.* Although there are probably exceptions to this rule, answering these questions in this order can help you purposefully plan for a lab experience.

Why do you need to grow your instructional leadership network?

There's no doubt that the principal is one of the most impactful sources of feedback and support for instruction in your building, but recognizing that they are part of a wider team that influences the building's culture is critical. Research around a distributed model of leadership "suggests that intervening to improve school leadership by focusing exclusively or chiefly on building the knowledge of an individual formal leader in a school may not be the most optimal or most effective use of resources" (Spillane, Halverson, & Diamond, 2001). Instead, it's important to recognize the influence of the many other individuals throughout the organization who contribute to its leadership.

Practically speaking, principals need help from a team. They need help building ownership among teachers so that new learning will be supported collaboratively, and they need help making connections between initiatives and stakeholders in order to form a coherent, cohesive approach to their vision. Fullan (2002) explains:

> An organization cannot flourish—at least, not for long—on the actions of the top leader alone. Schools and districts need many leaders at many levels. Learning in context helps produce such leaders. Further, for leaders to be able to deal with complex problems, they need many years of experience and professional development on the job. To a certain extent, a school leader's effectiveness in creating a culture of sustained change will be determined by the leaders he or she leaves behind.

So, if your reason for hosting a lab is rooted in supporting sustained change, and you're looking to help your principals build a team beyond their administrative colleagues who will help them do this, a lab to build a network of leaders can be a good fit.

What areas do you need support to strengthen?

Are you working on a particular aspect of your vision? Is there a problem of practice that you'd like to tackle with a collaborative approach? Does it relate specifically to an instructional area or to a broader culture? Determining that topic that you'd like team support in is critical because it may help you identify who you need to recruit.

When we set out to host labs to build a network of leaders, it was because the district we were working with was striving for sustained change in two main areas: the secondary schools were working on an instructional initiative around lesson design, and elementary schools were studying how to ensure that the CASEL (2020) competencies for social-emotional learning (SEL) were evident throughout instruction in culturally affirming ways rather than treated as a separate initiative. Both teams had already spent a good portion of time introducing these initiatives in their buildings, and now they wanted to study how to support this change in practice. Although principals and some teacher leaders had already done in-depth learning on their own, it was time to study how to move forward together as a network. Principals felt as though the SEL learning was still disconnected, and they wanted to expand their understanding to connect the work in authentic ways. They knew they needed to team up and build their network.

Once we named the *what* in our focus, we realized that the leaders we wanted to partner with would be teachers for our secondary schools and school social workers for the elementary. This would help give principals the right people to connect with to further their own learning and work in their buildings once the lab was over.

Who might you need to recruit?

Chances are, if your experience is anything like ours, you have a few people who come to mind automatically whenever you think of leadership opportunities. We found, though, that being intentional about expanding this list helped us gain traction, build ownership, and support more people more fully.

When we were working with secondary principals on developing instructional leadership around lesson design and collaboration, we knew we needed to think strategically about whose leadership would be the most effective. Simply asking for the teachers who traditionally volunteered for any leadership opportunity probably wouldn't get us a fit that was just right for supporting the work or partnering with the principals for this particular learning.

In order to help principals engage in reflection around who might be the best fit for this colearning, before the lab, we asked them to do a reflective activity to determine which teachers from their building they might want to attend the lab. To engage principals in thinking about who they might like to invite from their building, we adapted an activity from *School Culture Rewired* to ask principals to reflect on teachers' leadership capacity in terms of effectiveness around the lab's topic and influence. Gruenert and Whitaker (2015) explain, "In schools, teachers are the main repositories of the culture. Each teacher has a personality that contributes more or less to the strength of the culture. Some are very influential and some are hardly noticed. Other adults in the building, such as support staff, may also be influential in terms of affecting daily operations and the mood of the group" (p. 23). We wanted principals to take into consideration these nuances when determining who to invite.

We asked principals to divide a paper into four quadrants and to consider the horizontal axis "effectiveness" in terms of the change area we were studying and the vertical axis "influence" in terms of their influence on their peers (Figure 6.2). We then asked principals to consider which teachers might fall into the high influence and high effectiveness quadrants. Having this visual representation helped principals to see strengths that their staff had so that they could consider all candidates instead of the same few who traditionally jump at the chance.

FIGURE 6.2

Effectiveness Versus Influence

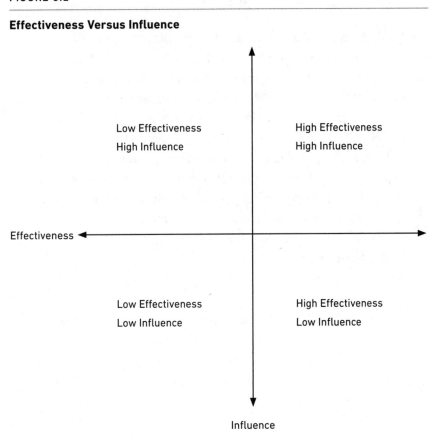

Low Effectiveness
High Influence

High Effectiveness
High Influence

Effectiveness

Low Effectiveness
Low Influence

High Effectiveness
Low Influence

Influence

Adapted from Gruenert & Whitaker, 2015.

Rather than give a formula for where on the graph teachers should be in order to be considered a good fit for the lab, we asked principals to make that determination while reflecting on questions like the following:

- What do you notice about this visual representation of your staff?
- Whose leadership might teachers in your building trust? Why might that be?
- In what ways might you want to grow the influence of someone who is effective in this area?
- In what ways might you want to grow the effectiveness of someone who is highly influential?

- Given this focus and what you know about your staff, is it better to invite someone highly effective or highly influential?
- In what ways have those who are effective or influential demonstrated that they value collaboration and ongoing learning?

This reflection activity was critical in preparing for a lab where we wanted to build instructional leadership networks with teaching staff, but we've also found that teachers aren't always the most appropriate leaders to invite to the lab. When we set out to plan for our lab studying the CASEL competencies, we knew that social workers were the leaders we wanted to work with. Their expertise was an invaluable lens into the work. Moreover, we recognized that these individuals in the building are highly impactful to our student population, but with their tightly scheduled days, there was rarely an opportunity for them to communicate with instructional staff, to plan with building principals, or even to connect with each other. Their leadership was critically important, and we needed to set aside a lab opportunity to learn how to integrate them into the system in collaboration with their building principals.

How will you build leadership through a lab experience?

Once you've answered the questions of *why, what,* and *who,* you're ready to start planning how you'll structure your lab through its major components: relationship building, anchoring experience, shared observation, and feedback and feeding forward.

Relationship Building

How might you lay the groundwork for teamwork?

One of the obvious benefits of having additional leaders on the team is that you get access to multiple perspectives, but this can also make communication a more complex process to navigate. Throughout the lab, it's essential to recognize differences in perspectives, to give feedback to one another, and for each participant to share their own understanding. At the heart of this communication is a relationship, which is why we decided to build upon the theme of communication in our relationship-building connectors for these labs.

Before you begin any of the usual components of a lab, you'll need to plan for some time to introduce the new leaders to the rest of the group. (This comes with the assumption that this is not your first principal lab and the usual participants already know one another.) Because it can be daunting for teachers, counselors, and other leaders to join a room full of principals and administrators, we knew that the first moments were important in putting them at ease and making them feel as though they were valuable participants in the day. Rather than having each new leader introduce themselves, we asked each principal participant to introduce the leader he or she brought and to share what strengths that person brings to the leadership team. This not only helped make the new teachers and social workers feel welcomed in the group, but it also helped the principals for whom the lab was designed to name and celebrate the leadership already happening in their buildings.

Once everyone had been introduced, we knew our connector activity would be a vehicle for laying the groundwork of communication for the group, so we chose back-to-back drawings. Participants had to stand back to back, and we distributed clipboards, blank paper, and cards with a given shape to each partnership. Taking turns, one partner explained to the other the shape that was on their card while the other attempted to draw it on their blank paper. After several instructions, the pairs then shared what the partner drew and compared it to the original image. Then they switched roles and tried again. We had each partnership take a couple of turns in each role so that they could debrief with each other and regroup about their communication strategy in between each turn.

After the activity, we asked participants to share what they learned as they progressed through the activity. We wanted them to reflect on the communication strategies they implemented to accurately reproduce the original drawing. Teams reflected on some important themes they needed in order to be successful communicating for a common goal, such as

- Listening to understand.
- Having a common understanding of the language.
- Learning from mistakes.
- Specificity.
- Clear step-by-step instructions.

We then lifted these themes to a broader conversation about successful communication and teamwork. Because the activity places participants back to back and they are therefore unable to provide feedback during the drawing process, debriefing provided us a natural segue into our day's focus as we talked about how important continuous communication and feedback are when you're working together toward a goal. We were also able to draw out the idea that every participant brings a different perspective. When we walk through our daily lives at school, we see and hear different things, and we process what we see and hear in different ways. Communicating each other's perspectives is crucial in order to move the work of systemic change forward.

Anchoring Experience

How do you engage participants authentically in shared learning?

In these labs you're building a crucial piece of your system, so it's important that this leadership component of the system reflects the same values as you're striving for with your instruction and students. For that reason, it was important to us that, while we work to build a shared understanding, we don't approach the learning as something to impart on our participants. We wanted to avoid the feeling of having learning done to those who attended this lab. In order to build a system that shared the values that we wanted for our students, we knew that we needed to engage participants in shared learning on some key principles: collaboration and ownership. To do this, we structured our anchoring experience with choice and facilitated discussion.

For our anchoring experience in our lab about building a network of leaders around instruction, we organized the participants into groups of four: a partnership made up of an administrator and leader from one school paired with another administrator and leader from another school. Pairing them across their typical building partnerships was important because we knew that a big component of the success of this lab was building a broader perspective of the system they were studying. We wanted principals to hear from the experiences and perspectives of administrators in other buildings so that they could better see how their own experiences fit within a bigger picture, and we wanted the newly invited leaders to start developing a perspective outside their own school so that they could broaden their leadership stance.

We provided everyone a choice of which article to read and after we gave a short overview of what they could expect from each article, we asked each pair of participants to decide which article they felt might best connect with what they were experiencing and problem-solving in their own buildings. Having an element of choice, even though it was controlled, was an important move in building agency in participants' learning because it gave them an opportunity to identify how the day's learning might best fit their own needs and perspectives.

To then process the reading, we wanted participants to engage in discourse. In *Culturally Responsive Teaching and the Brain,* Hammond and Jackson (2015) explain that "the classroom has to be designed around talk and task structures that allow students to define the people they see themselves becoming" (p. 148). In order to scale this to the leadership level of our system, we wanted an opportunity for dialogue that was open enough for participants to meaningfully process what they'd read yet facilitated enough that they would be able to safely participate in a way that helped them hear from multiple perspectives. To do this, we facilitated a modified jigsaw where each individual participant first paired with someone who had read the same article, then returned to their original partnership to craft a summary, and finally returned to their group of four to draw comparisons, find commonalities, and synthesize how the reading had furthered their thinking around the day's topic and the work in their buildings. Asking participants to move beyond their partnerships helped them get to know each other as they built a network and started to examine perspectives beyond their own comfort zones.

For our lab that sought to build leadership around the CASEL competencies, participants had already done quite a bit of shared learning on the competencies themselves, and they wanted to focus their learning on how to support the initiative as leaders. We, too, understood that our main charge was in digging into the *how* of leadership. So, we offered principals and their invited leaders a choice among a few different articles that explored the complexities of supporting change through various lenses. Reading and jigsawing the articles helped give participants a better understanding of the role that self-reflection, goal setting, and progress monitoring have on supporting change so that they could work as pairs to look through the lens of their own building and do some preliminary reflection and self-assessment before going into shared observations. By using these articles, we shifted the learning away from the content (CASEL competencies) and toward the participants' leadership capacities so that it was clear the day's learning would be about them. This was a crucial shift, as we wanted to ensure we weren't bringing in more people to tell other people what to do. Shifting the day's learning to how the principals and their invited guests can grow as leaders and as a team framed the lab to study how their own leadership can impact the systems in their buildings. Ultimately, principals appreciated the opportunity to discuss with their colleagues how to navigate the complexity of supporting change, and the lab served as a way to recharge and reframe their thinking as they planned their next steps in this process.

Shared Observations

How can you build perspective through observation?

Part of leadership is not being lost in your own practice, and so, to support this idea in our established and emerging leaders, we wanted all participants to build a wider perspective. In their "Survival Guide for Leaders," Heifetz and Linsky (2002) "call this skill 'getting off the dance floor and going to the balcony,' an image that captures the mental activity of stepping back from the action and asking, 'What's really going on here?'" In a sense, all principal labs work to build this balcony-level perspective by connecting principals to other administrators, observing in each other's buildings, and collaborating to learn about supporting initiatives. In these labs in particular, however, we were intentional in ensuring that all participants got "off the dance floor" for shared observations by requiring assigned partnerships to travel to buildings that weren't their own.

Because the purpose of this type of lab is to build that balcony-level view of specific initiatives or goals, we've found that we like to use learning looks as our mode for shared observation. These offer participants multiple shorter dips into classrooms to get a broader perspective of what's happening. To facilitate these smoothly, you can use any type or combination of learning look (structured, unstructured, or ghost visits) facilitation. In a lab to build a network of leaders where secondary principals were studying instruction alongside teacher leaders they had brought with them, we wanted participants to gain a broader perspective of what instruction looked like throughout their district. Middle and high school principals had already visited elementary buildings for a shared observation in an earlier lab, and they'd remarked about what an important experience it was for them and how they wished more secondary educators had a chance to see the instruction that their district's students were getting before they got to them in the secondary grades. So, for this lab, we wanted to position principals as sharing their new understanding with their developing leaders. For their observations, we assigned each partner group of principal and invited leader to a grade level, classroom, and elementary building. We structured the observations in this way to ensure that participants would see a wide range of classrooms, grade levels, and content lessons. This would help us build the wider leadership-oriented perspective we were striving for when the partnerships returned for whole-group discussion in the afternoon.

How do you organize observation notes?

Because our labs to build a network of leaders usually brought participants in to observe in buildings that weren't their own, we knew that it was easy for them to be overwhelmed by a new environment. When something is entirely outside the zone of what you're used to seeing, we found that it was easy to get distracted making connections or new realizations unrelated to the focus of the lab. For this reason, we made sure our observation templates were specific to the concept we were studying. For our lab with social workers, we listed each CASEL competency in a box and then, prior to the observation, we asked participants to brainstorm possible look-fors that would support each competency in the right column. Once they went into classrooms, they recorded observed evidence on the left (Figure 6.3). In the lab to study lesson design, we asked participants to make notes during specific chunks of time throughout the lesson. For each, we asked participants to list what they saw and heard.

We found that having a specific template helps keep both principals and their invited guests focused, and asking them to record what they see and hear lays the groundwork for appreciative inquiry because it primes participants to be ready to discuss what they *are* seeing, not what they *aren't* seeing. This is particularly important to us because we believe that it helps establish a culture for an asset-based approach throughout a building or district. If principals plan for support using what they see that people *can* do, they can better help teachers use the same approach, and teachers, in turn, can approach student support from an asset-based starting point. This appreciative inquiry approach is something that we regularly return to in all principal labs, but we knew that we wanted to be especially intentional about framing observations in this asset-based way as we worked to broaden our network of leaders. Because, for many of the principals' invited guests, this was an introduction to district-level leadership, we knew that it was important to introduce them to the district's culture for learning and leadership in concrete ways.

FIGURE 6.3

SEL Learning Looks Organizer

Evidence	Competency and Potential Look-Fors
	Self-Awareness
	Self-Management
	Social Awareness
	Relationship Skills
	Responsible Decision Making

How can the structure of your observation prepare participants for discussions?

We also found that, for this lab, it was particularly important to give observers each a distinct focus. Because principals, who typically are very comfortable with modes of observation, are pairing with teachers or other school leaders for whom observation may not be as familiar, it was important to us to set up the partnerships so that both felt they had something to bring to the discussion. To do this, when they went into the classroom for their observations, we asked administrators to focus on what they saw the students saying and doing, and we asked their partners to focus on the teacher in the room. You could choose to focus each partner in a variety of different ways, but we knew that asking them to each take ownership of their own experience would be important. This way, we would lessen the possibility of power dynamics if a principal and teacher pairing saw something differently. Having focused on different aspects of the experience, instead of disagreeing, they could build their conversation around their varying perspectives, which we tied back to our takeaways from our connector. For the invited guests, this was important because it helped build their efficacy in feeling like they had something to contribute to the post-observation discussion. And for the principals at the lab, it was important to expand their observation experience to consider multiple perspectives so that they could also develop their own breadth and depth as instructional leaders.

Feedback and Feeding Forward

How can you structure discussions that will help identify the next steps forward within a safe culture for learning?

It can be easy to be critical of a building that isn't your own sometimes, so we've found that when we're observing in buildings that aren't our own, it's especially important to build the culture of asset-based learning. Cooperrider and Whitney (2005) explain the appreciative inquiry (AI) approach: "Instead of negation, criticism, and spiraling diagnosis, there is discovery, dream, and design. AI involves the art and practice of asking unconditionally positive questions that strengthen a system's capacity to apprehend, anticipate, and heighten positive potential" (p. 8). Regardless of the trust you've built with principals, bringing new leaders who don't identify as administrators into the conversation can complicate this dynamic, and it was crucial to us to continue to build leadership within a system that positively builds capacity and potential. So, although appreciative inquiry is always important, during this lab, keeping observation conversations in an asset-based stance is even more critical. To do this, we used the following structures, which helped principals by rooting them in good work that was already underway so that they could continue to build momentum with their invited leaders and maximize impact.

Paired Perspectives. If you asked participants to focus on either the teacher or the students during their observation, giving them a chance to compare notes to share what they saw and heard in the classroom can be a powerful way to debrief. We asked participants to name what they each saw and heard and to make inferences about how their individual observations might connect to each other and under what conditions they may continue to yield positive results.

Observation Sort. Either following the paired perspectives or on its own, you may choose to have your participants analyze their observations and prime the pump for planning by engaging them in an observation sort. To do this, we asked partnerships to list on individual sticky notes any observations they made. This should be done by what they saw and heard, not by what they felt might have been missing, in order to keep the analysis in an asset-based space. Once they named their observations on sticky notes, we moved to an open space (a blank whiteboard, a wall of lockers, etc.), and partnerships grouped their sticky notes in order to find trends. Once they named some trends, we asked the group to self-reflect on the celebrations that were emerging and where they might be identifying goals for their own buildings. This was helpful from a networking perspective because those who identified a goal in one building could connect with those who found success in a similar one in another building.

Plan and Connect. Sorting their observations into celebrations and goals helped our participants move into a planning space, but in order to make that planning more concrete, we found it helpful to make concrete connections to the planning for this work. To do this, we asked participants to review their most current school improvement plans, and then we used a discussion protocol to ask them to reflect on their current reality as it relates to the day's learning.

Small Wins. Change can take time, so we've found that it's important not to wait until you've reached an end goal to celebrate an achievement. In his book *Leading Change in Your School,* Douglas B. Reeves (2009) explains, "Without short-term wins, the pain of change often overwhelms the anticipated long-term benefits" (p. 92). In line with this, it's important to recognize success along the way. In our work with principal labs, we've called this "small wins," and during our feedback and feeding forward portion of the day, we work to identify some of those small wins and plan for how to communicate them to the staff so that they can share in that celebration and avoid being overwhelmed.

Collaborative Planning. At the end of these labs, we provided time for the principals and their invited guest (in our case, teachers and social workers) to plan together for how they would take this experience back to their own buildings. Up to this point, the discussion had been heavily facilitated, so we gave them time and a few guiding questions:

- Based on your thinking today, what might be the next steps for your building?
- How and when might this work take place?

To facilitate these discussions, we shifted back and forth between having participants talk in partnerships, with larger table groups, and as a whole group. This was important because, while we were working to build the relationship between the partnerships of leaders within the building, we understood that great strength also came from the larger network and the cross-building collaboration. While they worked together, participants made plans for structuring PLC meetings, facilitating professional learning during staff meetings, and additional learning on their part.

How might you continue to support the network once the lab is over?

Because principal labs are situated within a system for professional learning, most principal labs include some opportunity to follow up with participants after the lab has ended. Whether this happens during a regularly scheduled administration meeting, instructional rounds, or surveys, we usually had some opportunity to get a sense of how participants were bringing the learning back to their buildings and what their next steps might be. Because this type of lab involves participants who don't typically attend administration meetings and who we are intentionally trying to weave into the system of support, we knew that we needed to intentionally plan to follow up with the leaders who were invited to these principal labs. A few weeks after the labs, we invited participants to join us for an opportunity to process and reflect on what they'd experienced. We made this an optional opportunity and found that it helped to survey when they'd like to attend (after school hours or during school with substitute coverage if necessary). Because these leaders were not members of the administrative team, and for many of them, this may have been their first opportunity to step into a leadership role alongside principals, we understood that there were power dynamics that could affect reflection. So, for the optional session, we chose to only invite the leaders who were not our regular principal lab participants. This gave them an opportunity to process their experience and think more deeply about their role in the change process alongside their colleagues who share similar roles and perspectives as they do. This optional follow-up was important for us because it helped us better understand how to support our new leaders and the change they were supporting, and it was important for them to reflect on their experience and their next steps moving forward.

Another way that we have sought to continue to strengthen the networks that are built in these labs is through establishing and strengthening committees or small collaborative groups. During a secondary lab that worked to build a network of leaders who could support learning around collaboration in instruction, principals worked together with their invited leaders to plan the next steps for professional learning. They valued having teachers' perspectives, and as they brought their plans back to their buildings, they realized that, though it was undoubtedly helpful to have this broader network, it was difficult to continue to dedicate that time for collaboration on their own. So, administrators and teacher leaders proposed a collaborative partnership to continue planning monthly staff meetings. The group was smaller than the total participants who attended the lab to build a network of leaders, but with that lab as a shared experience, they were able to continue to grow the work. At least one principal and one of the teacher leaders who attended the lab from each building came together after school to share their perspectives of how the last professional learning had gone, what they were noticing since then, and to plan the next step. These monthly meetings were far shorter than a principal lab (an hour each, typically), but they served as a continuation of the learning. We have also found that it's helpful to continue to facilitate these meetings through a lens of appreciative inquiry where members share what they're noticing is going well. This is helpful because it focuses on continuing the momentum and the culture you build in the lab experiences.

Beyond the initial optional follow-up meeting with invited leaders, we recommend that you look for additional opportunities to weave these leaders into your system for support. Whether that means they attend another lab, are invited to participate in school improvement committees, or attend planning meetings for professional learning offerings, their perspective continues to be an important one to draw upon. For principals we've worked with, having expanded their network by inviting additional leaders into the work of planning helped in the brainstorming and collaboration stages of planning, but having more individuals able to lead the work also made their plans for facilitating in both small and large groups nimble, and they were able to gain more traction in their plans than if they'd continued without their expanded cohorts.

The Heart of the Lab

This lab works to enact the belief that "the notion of leaders as 'heroes' must be dispelled and replaced with a collaborative approach" (Sawyer & Stukey, 2019). In it, you're bringing together participants of varying roles and perspectives to study a system for sustained change. Getting into each other's buildings for shared observations helped participants of all roles gain new perspectives so that they can take ownership of the learning and bring it back to their home buildings. It's an important lab for building a collaborative, asset-based culture, for strengthening your system, and for supporting emerging leaders. Labs to build a network of leaders emerged for us in a way that was almost unplanned. We knew our work toward sustained change was daunting, we knew we needed more hands on deck, and we decided to experiment with the principal lab structure that we'd grown familiar with, so we invited new leaders into the mix. Although our labs to build a network of leaders were almost spontaneous, we believe that they are an enduring and important type of principal lab.

FIGURE 7.1

Aspirations Sample Agenda

Principal Lab Agenda
Aspirations

Morning

Relationship Building
- Connector: Breakout EDU
- Points of Pride: What are your points of pride?

Anchoring Experience
- Choice Article
- Thinking Partners: What are your future points of pride that are your "works in progress"?
- Forming Topics: Sticky Note Sort

Shared Observation
- Groupings
- Visit a building to explore a future point of pride "work in progress."

Lunch

Afternoon

Feedback and Feeding Forward
- Cross-Dialogue
- School Improvement Plan Connections

Aspire Closing
- Celebrations and Commitments

Adapted with permission from Waterford School District.

7

Labs to Foster Collaborative Aspirations

When you look at the research that has been shaping professional learning for the past few years, two factors are emerging as having a particularly significant impact on designing professional learning that will stick: collaboration and an inquiry-based approach. While all principal labs cultivate these two practices, labs to foster collaborative aspirations especially equip participants to take on this work with autonomy. That's because these labs are designed for principals to purposefully build their networks around areas of inquiry that they are interested in applying to their work.

These labs are driven by participant need and are rooted in collaboration. Rather than planning a curricular or instructional focus ahead of time, you'll lead participants to decide the focus on the spot. For this reason, these labs are immediately responsive to the needs of the individuals in the group.

As a facilitator for these labs, preparing content is not your priority. Instead, your planning energy will go into facilitation moves that skillfully group participants and engage them in appreciative inquiry in safe, brave spaces of learning.

In reflecting on our years of facilitating principal labs and how we might share them with others, we realize that there may be an inclination to start with this type of lab. They allow for the most differentiation, and in many ways, they are similar to the instructional rounds structure, which your participants may already be familiar with. Although this may be tempting, we believe that we found success with this type of lab only once we had a shared vision around what instruction should look like and had built a culture for collaborative learning around instructional leadership through other types of principal labs.

Likewise, we believe we were only successful with this type of lab where the content and focus are decided on the spot because we had grown so much as facilitators through the course of principal labs. Because of the impromptu nature, we've learned that the facilitation moves must be tighter than usual to ensure that the learning experience is equitable and truly responsive.

Even though you may not be planning ahead for shared content, it is absolutely imperative to pre-plan facilitation for each component of the lab. See Figure 7.1 for a sample agenda for an aspirations lab.

Relationship Building

How do you plan to celebrate what's going well?

Points of pride is a consistent structure in every lab; participants come to expect it. Although it can take many different forms, from building tours to highlighting one particular celebration to sharing in small groups, for this lab, we knew we had to be especially intentional because the points of pride would anchor much of the day's trajectory. When we emailed participants to schedule this lab, we also asked them to prepare a point of pride that represented something they felt their building had been really working on and was finally showing some signs of accomplishment. We knew that, because this lab would ask principals to dig in and get vulnerable to study something that might not feel like an accomplishment yet, it would be important to set the tone by reinforcing a feeling of success.

Once principals were together, during our time reserved for points of pride, we asked each participant to briefly share the accomplishment. These were not formal presentations but rather just quick verbal share-outs around a circle as we started our day. As each participant took their turn, we had one person record a brief summary of the point of pride from each building. We anchored these to the front of the room and let the group know that they may return to these at some point to make connections later in the day. We also sent these out with a follow-up email after the lab so that they could quickly refer to them when continuing to think about possible networking opportunities.

How can participants deepen their understanding of what it takes to be part of a collaborative team?

We facilitated this lab after participants were already growing to know each other fairly well, so we knew we didn't need a light icebreaker connector to build relationships, but we did want to connect them to one of the day's major focuses: collaboration. We also facilitated this lab in January. In Michigan, this means that everyone has been enduring seemingly nonstop gray skies, frigid temperatures, and the weight of mid-year testing, so we knew we wanted something that would provide relief and much-needed levity.

To do this, we broke participants into separate teams for a virtual breakout room. We purposefully divided the participants up so that they would mix with people they don't usually work with. For us, this was a K–12 lab, so we made sure some elementary principals were paired with high school principals and that buildings from across town got to work together.

Because this lab wasn't focusing on any one piece of content, we selected a premade breakout room that incorporated many different types of challenges: mathematical clues, word puzzles, and visual challenges. The experience brought people out of their comfort zones, and everyone contributed unique perspectives. During the challenge, there was plenty of laughter and competition, and afterward, we made sure to debrief with the group about how their experience might connect to the day's lab. We've found that this debrief is often a key component to ensuring the connector is, indeed, doing its job of connecting to the day's learning and doesn't just seem like a standalone activity. To do this, we asked participants to reflect on what they learned from their experience about working collaboratively as a group. They shared observations like the following:

- Make sure to ask to hear from people who see it differently.
- Explaining your thinking helps.
- Sometimes the obvious option isn't the right one.
- Don't be afraid to try something new.

As participants lifted these in discussion, we recorded and anchored them to extend on our group's norms for collaborative work.

Anchoring Experience

How might you anchor participants in a shared experience when they will be choosing different areas of focus to study?

For this lab, rather than content, curriculum, or particular instructional strategies, we anchored ourselves in the idea of working together for systemic change. That's because this lab isn't about coming together around a common *what;* it's about digging into *how* we learn and lead together. For this lab, principals wouldn't be focusing on what they saw teachers doing; they'd study how they can work together collaboratively with each other to sustain their initiatives.

Because this is not as concrete an idea to anchor participants in as, say, a new science curriculum, we needed to think in terms of the members of our team and what ideas they needed common language around in order to build the collaborative networks needed to really support them as instructional leaders. So, we sought out articles to engage participants that would provide a foundation for discussion. We knew that connecting the new to known would be important, so one of those articles focused on the practice of using instructional rounds. We knew that some members of the team had engaged in learning around these before and had found some success, so we purposefully chose this article to lay the groundwork and base discussion in how to extend from familiarity with instructional rounds as a starting point. We also knew that one of the ideas we needed to build upon was the idea of collaboration. In a large district of several schools, administrators often found themselves feeling a bit as though they were on an island—or, worse yet, as though they were in competition with one another. (In these labs, we frequently referred to a common district saying that we were striving to "be a school district instead of a district of schools.") To anchor participants in learning and discussion around the concept of collaboration, we chose an article on collaborative teams from the business sector. These two topics worked well for our group because they grew from what we had learned about participants in previous labs, but as you are planning for this type of lab in your own schools, we encourage you to look for shared readings that will anchor your participants in an experience that will help them better improve the *how* of working together for systemic change.

During the lab, we gave participants the choice of which article to read, and then we engaged them in a discussion protocol to unpack their thinking together. For our discussion, we used the Four *A*'s discussion protocol from School Reform Initiative (2017a). In this protocol, as participants read, they annotate around the following areas of focus:

- What *assumptions* does the author of the text hold?
- What do you *agree* with in the text?
- What do you want to *argue* with in the text?
- What parts of the text do you want to *aspire* to?

Although we often find that protocols for discussion about text can be somewhat interchangeable, in this case, this particular protocol was important. First, it honors readers' experiences with the article by assuming that they may agree with or argue with the author's ideas. We also would transition to the next component of the day by expanding on their thinking in the "aspire" category.

Determining Focus

How can you support participants in determining a focus that will be meaningful for them?

Typically, before anything else about a lab, facilitators plan the focus ahead of time. But for this lab, the participants determine the focus during the course of your facilitation. For this reason, it's crucial that your facilitation supports them choosing something that is meaningful so that participants walk away feeling as though it was a good use of their valuable time.

To ensure that principals were choosing focus areas of study that were meaningful, we wanted them to identify topics that were relevant and challenging yet attainable. They needed to be relevant so that principals felt like they were engaging in learning that they could immediately use and bring back to their buildings and the teachers they support, and they needed to be challenging (yet attainable) so that they would find collaboration to be valuable. In other words, we wanted them to choose meaty problems of practice, not something surface level or logistical that they just hadn't had time to think through yet. We suspected that simply asking them to select a topic would not be supportive enough. First, selecting a topic like this involves an inherent vulnerability. Participants have to say that they want help thinking through something that they don't have an answer for. And second, you want them to feel buoyed by the topic they choose and their collaborative team, not weighed down by something so difficult it seems insurmountable. So, to tackle this difficult facilitation, we connected our discussion back to our points of pride and to the "aspire" from their text-based discussion protocol.

To cultivate a culture where participants can be open to new learning, it is important to start this conversation by focusing on what is working well. It stems from an appreciative inquiry approach, which focuses on "strengths and opportunities" rather than problems and deficits (Henderson et al., 2011). First, we asked participants to independently reflect on the point of pride they shared earlier in the day. They might think about what factors may have contributed to its success or about indicators they had along the way that helped them know they were on the right track. Then, we asked them to reflect on what ways those markers of success connected to the ideas they lifted from their reading. We recommend debriefing this reflection as a whole group to bring to the forefront a strength-based approach to their upcoming inquiry.

Then, we connected back to the fourth *A* in the discussion protocol: aspire. We asked participants to reflect on what they are aspiring to, or more specifically, "What are your future points of pride that are a work in progress right now?" This framed their topics in a positive, hopeful light that was consistent with a structure for celebrating success that was well-established in our culture for learning. Cooperrider and Whitney (2005) explain, "Human systems grow in the direction of what they persistently ask questions about, and this propensity is strongest and most sustainable when the means and ends of inquiry are positively correlated" (p. 9).

For this facilitation, we distributed large sticky notes to each participant and coordinated which color they received by their grade level. For example, principals in a K–5 building got one color while principals in 6–8 and 9–12 buildings got different colors. This helped us see trends and notice when initiatives spanned across grade levels so that participants could approach their collaboration from a systems perspective. Once each participant had recorded one aspiring point of pride on their respective sticky notes, we asked each to share and stick their note to the wall. As they did this, participants began to sort their aspirations into categories of similar initiatives. As sticky notes of varying colors (and thus levels) became grouped together, we were able to think in terms of celebrating throughout a system to explore how we could support each other to get stronger.

Once all the sticky notes were sorted, we asked the groups to collectively name each category. They came up with several examples, including intervention, student engagement, and restorative practices. The sticky notes within these categories, then, would determine the membership of each collaborative group and their focus for the remainder of the day.

Shared Observation

How do you choose where to observe?

For most other labs, the facilitators determine ahead of time which classrooms participants will visit, but for this lab, each group determined which building or buildings to visit for their shared observations. Because we asked them to choose something that was a future point of pride, or a work in progress, we knew that they were identifying something that they'd already begun to think about and potentially implement steps toward.

Once groups were together and before they set out for their inquiry, we asked them some open-ended questions to guide their initial discussion toward refining their topic and deciding where to go for their shared observation. Questions that you might consider include the following:

- Why did you identify this as a future point of pride?
- What about this have you found some success with?
- What about this topic makes you want to ask more questions?
- What might you need to see in action in order to get a better idea of what your next steps might be?

How might you approach the observation itself?

The observations themselves are another reason we were glad to have started implementing this type of lab once the culture and process was already well established. Participants were already familiar with how observations worked and how to step out of evaluation mode and toward taking an appreciative, learning stance toward their observations.

To help participants tie their observations to their initial inquiry, we designed a loosely structured grid to drive their collaborative conversations (Figure 7.2). In the top left corner, participants recorded questions they identified when discussing their topics of inquiry. Group members could choose to record all of their group's questions or only those that particularly resonate with their own trajectory. Then, in the next box, they had space to take notes while in observations. The bottom two boxes, then, were reserved to structure their group's discussion that would follow the observation: shifts in thinking and takeaways or next steps. We thought that even though these boxes would be filled out during the feedback and feeding forward portion of the lab, it was important that participants know about them beforehand and have them at the front of their minds throughout the observation.

Feedback and Feeding Forward

Even though we didn't know what exactly each group would choose to study in their lab experience, we knew it was important to support their analysis of what they saw, so we used some of the following protocols to structure the discussion once participants returned from their chosen observations.

"If, Then" Frame

We found that this traditional frame is helpful for analyzing participants' observations and moving into a planning stance. With this frame, participants use their observation notes to notice trends and develop hypotheses that outline cause-and-effect relationships. For example, if they chose a topic of inquiry around engagement because they knew their students were struggling with textbook-based engagement, and in their observations, they noticed that students in classes that were experiential or problem-based had higher levels of engagement, they may develop a hypothesis to the effect of "If I lead a teacher inquiry cohort on PBL, then they may see increased engagement in their classes."

FIGURE 7.2

Aspirations Observation Template

Focus: Intervention in Elementary Classrooms

Questions/Wonders	Notes
• How can teachers pull small groups while keeping the whole class engaged? • How does tier one instruction support students who might also need additional support? • How and when do students get identified as needing additional support? • How can we provide more targeted support to students who need additional help?	Building A: Observed Two Classrooms • Ss working in small groups on common math task. • T circulates through room; returns frequently to Group 1. • Ss use a variety of manipulatives and strategies. • T refers to charts and visuals in room. Building B: Observed MTSS Student Team Meeting • Present: Social worker, special ed teacher, EL teacher, classroom teacher, administrator, paraprofessional. • Social worker facilitates and charts notes from discussion visibly. • Norms include guidance around each person participating, timing for components of discussion. • Discussion: Identify problems, root cause analysis, possible solutions, prioritize, necessary resources.
Shifts in My Thinking	Takeaways/Next Steps
• Engage students in the same task but provide additional differentiated supports. • We need a protocol in place for facilitating MTSS student team meetings. • Part of MTSS discussion is around resources: who to involve, train, etc. We can use MTSS meetings to guide professional learning planning.	• Teachers need training on manipulatives and strategies; ask Ms. Brown if she will video or host a lab for her K–2 team. • Inventory manipulatives. • Develop MTSS team and train in protocol. • Develop process for connecting MTSS to PL planning to support teachers and paraprofessionals in necessary differentiation.

Dyad and Triad Debriefing

This stage of the debrief asks participants to process what they saw in their chosen observations by talking with multiple mixed groups of participants. The point here was that we wanted everyone to have the opportunity to not only further process what they were studying but to also metacognitively reflect on how their inquiry was taking shape. Because our anchoring experience was focused on systemic change, we wanted to ensure that their individual topics of inquiry didn't become isolated; instead, we wanted participants to make connections and begin to shape their plans within their greater system.

Exactly how you mix up your groups will depend on the number of people involved. For ours, we first split everyone up into dyads: two people from the same level (elementary, middle, high) but who were in different inquiry groups. Then, we moved them into triads of mixed levels and different inquiry groups. Once in those groups, we asked some guiding questions to prompt their discussion. Again, how exactly you craft those questions may depend on the dynamics of your group, but some general questions that we have asked in the past include the following:

- What was your observation focus?
- Where did you go? What did you notice?
- How did what you see connect to what you're doing in your buildings?
- What is lingering with you as a result of your visits?

After these intentionally mixed groups, we asked participants to return to their original inquiry group to think systemically about next steps. We asked questions to get them started that included the following:

- What similarities did you hear from other group members during your cross-dialogue?
- What connections are you making?
- What is lingering with you after hearing other groups' experiences?
- What might be some next steps for us as a group? To connect with other groups?

Through this dialogue, group members were able to process and reflect on their own learning and experiences, and they began to see connections between their inquiry topic and others to think systemically toward next steps for their own learning and planning for action. If you're facilitating these labs, you likely won't know ahead of time exactly what the areas of inquiry will be, and there's no way of knowing what connections may surface. To plan for this to happen, structuring discussion in multiple varied groups helped us shape discourse that would make for meaningful reflection.

School Improvement Plan Connections

In this lab, participants choose one area of inquiry, and they study it deeply. For a leader to leave this lab feeling like they either have only this one area of study to focus on or must devote the same depth and level of inquiry to everything that crosses their desk would be unrealistic. Instead, we felt it was important to help principals better understand the interconnected nature of their areas of learning. To help them plan forward within this network, we followed the dyad and triad debriefing by bringing participants together as a whole group. We said, "Today, we were studying *a* thing (singular). Now let's take a look at the things (plural) that are important to you as instructional leaders." We then asked participants to write each of these important things down on individual sticky notes. Then we invited everyone up to stand around a large piece of blank butcher paper, share their sticky notes one at a time, and place them on the paper. As they found similarities in the things that were important, they started to group their sticky notes, and categories started to form. Once these categories were taking shape and all sticky notes had been shared, we asked the group, "What connections do you see? What might this mean as you draft your school improvement plans for next year?" As they pointed out connections, we recorded their thinking by drawing lines between the groups of sticky notes and labeling potential school improvement goals and actions. As the conversation progressed, a web or net started to take shape to visually represent the networks they were forming through the lab's discussion. They began discussing strategies and resources they were considering as they ventured into their plans for the coming year. That then led to principals teaming up to tackle the work together between their buildings. The discussion was understated with a fairly simple facilitation and basic resources like sticky notes, a piece of paper, and a marker, but it yielded great value as principals saw their school improvement work move beyond a formality and into the heart of what was important to them. And to help them tackle this important work from a systemic standpoint, principals began to form partnerships to support each other's school improvement goals.

Book Study

This was something that started organically in one of our labs. As participants in one of the groups discussed their observations and plans for moving forward, they determined that one of their next steps was to continue with some shared learning, so they identified a book that they'd like to read and planned to come together for book club discussions in the upcoming weeks. The extended learning connected to their lab experience in such an authentic way that we decided to offer a selection of optional book clubs in future labs to foster collaborative aspirations and continue and extend the inquiry established within the lab.

Aspire Closing

Moving beyond what's happening now and shifting the focus toward future steps is one of the most important parts of this lab. Because it doesn't have the predesigned focus that other types of principal labs do, it is easy for these labs to feel like instructional rounds, focusing on what is happening rather than on the feedback and feeding forward component of a lab. Each step in this section of the lab was critical for this reason, and we decided to wrap up the lab by tying it back to the theme we'd started with: aspirations. We brought this word back from our Four *A*'s reading protocol, and we asked participants to reflect first on what made them identify that aspiration as an inquiry for the day and then on how their experience in the lab would affect their learning and plans moving forward.

To facilitate this closing reflection, you might ask questions grounded in appreciative inquiry like the following:

- Reflect on your chosen topic of inquiry: What is going well so far? Why do you think that might be? Where do you aspire to go next? How might you build upon success you've already experienced?
- How will today's learning experience influence the work you'll be doing in your building in the coming days, weeks, and months?

However you might word or structure your closing reflection, it's important to ground everyone in things that they're starting to work on, building on successes along the way, and determining next steps to continue the learning.

The Heart of the Lab

When you facilitate this type of principal lab, you're ultimately releasing responsibility to participants. Though you're still supporting the process through thoughtfully planned facilitation, they will drive the focus of what they're studying. Because of this, this type of lab can at times feel more hands-off, and we were initially worried that we would be able to balance giving everyone autonomy and having them find it useful. We found, though, that it was a perfect way to cap off a series of principal labs because it built upon the culture that we'd worked so hard as a team to develop, and it empowered everyone to carry on with purposeful, collaborative, and appreciative inquiry as a part of how they do business as an instructional leader.

8

Logistics

When we first started facilitating principal labs, we didn't intentionally differentiate between planning for different types of labs. Instead, we leaned into the overall structure and let relationship building and participants' feedback shape how we'd focus our labs for the day. From this emerged the different types of labs described in this book. Regardless of the type of lab, though, there are logistical moves that have helped us make principal labs run smoothly and sustain learning beyond the scheduled labs. Because they run throughout all types of labs and throughout the overall structure, these universal logistics can be categorized into how we understand the needs of the lab structure and participants.

Logistics for Scheduling

There are no hard and fast rules for scheduling a principal lab, but since relationship building is a primary goal, a one-and-done approach won't work. Instead, they should be implemented as a series, meaning that they occur periodically throughout the school year. Likewise, because the work is so complex and important, we recommend that you set aside a full day for each lab. With so many busy schedules, this can be a hard sell at first, but doing so will help establish that instructional leadership is a priority in your school and is worth the investment.

In Chapter 3, we discussed this shared belief that our own learning is valuable and thus worth the investment. To simply say we value it is not enough, though. We've found that it's important to build this shared belief by carefully planning in ways that show participants you value their time. Some ways that we've done this include the following:

- **Think holistically about your calendar.** Principal labs shouldn't be isolated events, which means you'll want more than one each year. (We often found that three or four per year was just right for us.) As you start planning, look at the whole school year calendar to decide when these labs might have the biggest impact and when principals will be best able to attend to their own learning. For example, if you know that spirit week or preparing for state testing especially pulls on an administrator's attention, try to avoid scheduling principal labs in the weeks surrounding those events.
- **If your group is large enough, offer two dates for the same lab.** If you have more than one principal or administrator in your building, you want them all to be able to attend labs, but it can be nearly impossible for everyone to be out of the building at the same time. Having the same lab run twice in a row allows half of a building's administrators to be out at a time, leaving the others to be available in their buildings.
- **Consider a system for developing substitutes for when administrators are out.** This is a great opportunity to build leadership opportunities for teachers in your district. Having a systematic way of identifying go-to substitute administrators in your teaching staff can be a relief on principal lab days and for the many other times that administrators are called out of their buildings.
- **Schedule full-day labs with grace time at the beginning and end.** The depth of learning that goes on within a principal lab means the agenda will almost always last for a full day, but we've found that defining a "whole day" different from the contractual hours was helpful. Because principals have so many pieces in play around arrival and dismissal time, we found that scheduling our labs with a start time of half an hour after the start of a school day and an end time half an hour before the school's dismissal allowed participants to get back to their buildings if needed or tie up loose ends over email or with staff from their buildings.
- **Include scheduled breaks in the norms of your meetings.** Principals get a lot of emails and phone calls throughout a school day, and attending to those can distract participants. Acknowledge

this from the outset and affirm your shared recognition that both the emails and the learning are important by scheduling 15-minute breaks throughout your day (at least one in the morning and one in the afternoon) so that participants can attend to their email or phone calls during that time and be more present throughout the lab. To be sure, they'll have some catching up to do after the lab, but the breaks allow them to triage what's coming in, and it sends the message that you know they have other needs to attend to.

- **Be thoughtful about lunch options.** We all know that it's a good day when principals feel like they have enough time to actually eat the lunch they packed, so we have found that honoring lunch as a necessity is important for taking care of participants' wellness. This can mean reserving a restaurant table and ensuring the whole party can get in and out within a reasonable time, taking orders ahead of time and coordinating a delivery, or simply allotting enough time and pointing participants in the direction of the nearest options. Planning ahead for how participants will eat lunch is a small but meaningful gesture to show participants that you care about their well-being—something that is pivotal to building relationships.

- **Model the importance of learning through all participants.** You already know how important it is to have administrators from central office as participants so that you have aligned support throughout the system. They, too, must model the importance of learning for leaders by prioritizing their time in labs. When a principal sees his or her superior pop in and out of the lab to take phone calls or attend other meetings, it sets the tone that the learning really isn't all that important for all leaders.

Who to Invite

In the midst of the school year, it seems like every day turns into a hectic one and time is at a premium, so it's tempting to try to divide and conquer. As with all principal labs, though, we'd strongly recommend that you treat this professional learning as premium time. All principal labs offer an opportunity to build community and shared learning between your colleagues, but Stein and Nelson's (2003) research on content understanding for administrators offers additional reasons to have every administrator all-in for labs that introduce new curriculum. If, for example, you're studying a new curriculum that is being implemented in the 9th grade, at a minimum, every high school administrator should attend. If it builds upon work being done at another level, you may want to consider inviting principals from that level as well. Having middle school and high school principals together, for example, can offer an opportunity to build understanding of how to support students as they transition within each content area.

Likewise, if you have curriculum coaches or consultants in your district, ISD, or region who are supporting the teachers through the process, their attendance—and insight during the planning stages—will be crucial.

It's also important to have administrators from the central office participate alongside the principals. Just as teachers feel vulnerable and need to know that their evaluators are getting the same message as they are, building principals do, too. Having a shared vision and message across all roles and levels is key to ensuring that everyone feels supported in taking risks.

Location

Depending on whether you're planning for a lab for an individual school or a larger district, principals may or may not be observing classrooms in their own buildings, but they should be in classrooms that are directly applicable to their own practice. This means that, most often, secondary principals will group together with other secondary principals to learn about and observe instruction in secondary classrooms in their district. This is not to say that the experience is limited to homogeneous grouping, though. If, for example, a district's high school principals would benefit from seeing what instruction looks like in the schools that feed into theirs, expanding the experience beyond secondary classrooms would be an effective way to focus the lab.

If everyone in the lab will be observing classrooms in the same building, we've found that asking that building to host the whole principal lab is helpful. Doing so, and rotating which buildings take on this hosting role, helps every member of an administrative team feel like a part of a whole district as they get to know each other's buildings. It also helps to streamline your timing if everyone is already in the same building. We found for some labs, though, that hosting everything but the shared observations in a more neutral location (like a central office) was helpful. We chose to do this when we asked groups to spread out to a variety of buildings for their shared observations. This way, they'd bring what they saw back to the learning space of the lab as equal participants.

Logistics for Structuring the Lab Space

When you're facilitating a principal lab, you're often at the mercy of the building's available space—which can be limited at best. So, when thinking about structuring the space for principal labs in general, we try to be as open-minded and flexible as possible. Sometimes, you roll with it to make just about anything work. But, just as classroom teachers work to ensure that their spaces are optimized for learning, the same is true when facilitating principal labs. Regardless of the specifics or limitations of the space, we have found it's important to be intentional about three main concepts.

1. Arrange participants' seating in a way that serves the focus of the lab.

If, for example, you are studying collaborative learning, placing participants into small, collaborative groups will help facilitate their own collaborative interactions. If you're studying restorative practices, start the day in a restorative circle. If you're studying an element of instructional technology, like breakout rooms or collaborative whiteboards, ensure everyone is able to engage as participants.

2. When in doubt, start in a circle.

As you break into different groups for specific discussions, of course you can expect your participants to move beyond this space, but having a circle as the basis of your structure puts everyone on equal footing visually so that you can honor the depth of discussion and participants' own vulnerability. Being able to see everyone's face throughout the discussion also helps personalize the conversation. Especially when it's not your own building, it's too easy to blindly critique without considering the human element of the learning process. Likewise, building principals can be so personalized that they are too defensive to recognize the teachers as learners. Facing each other throughout the whole-group discussion can help establish the tone.

3. Keep learning visible.

Throughout the day, as you chart discussions, keep the posters up even if you move on to a new discussion. Likewise, organize texts and handouts into a folder or onto a clipboard that you can easily reference. Depending on the group's dynamics, you may do this with paper, digital copies, or both. Regardless of how you keep the handouts organized, it's important to build a little bit of time into the pace of your agenda to adequately help participants navigate each item as you reference it. Keeping artifacts and resources at your fingertips and at your eye level will help ground the discussion to your focus and lift it for participants to make connections to their new learning.

Logistics for the Host

Communication with Host Teachers

No matter what your timing is, it is absolutely essential that when beginning principal labs any teachers you plan to visit know well in advance that you're coming. Again, this is not so that they can prepare something special for their visitors or put on their best show. Instead, they need to have a full understanding of your purpose so they know that your presence is not evaluative; in fact, it's the opposite. They should go into the experience with the understanding that you are trying to learn how to better support them.

When you're coming. What dates will you be coming in? During which blocks of time? Make sure they know to expect you for the whole lesson.

Who will be there. Although it might not be possible or entirely necessary to share the name of every leader who will visit their room, teacher participants should have a broad understanding of who the attendees will be. Saying something like, "In addition to myself, we'll have principals from our other high school and the middle school joining us" will give teachers a better context for who the unfamiliar faces are in their classroom.

What to expect of lesson participants. Share with teachers your norms for observing so that they understand that the lab participants are not there to interact with students or interfere with the lesson in any way.

The purpose of your lab. Since you understand that teachers who are taking this on are experiencing a sense of insecurity, it is more than appropriate to share that you, too, are using this as a learning experience. Talk with them about what learning edges you will be working on and how this can help them in the long run.

Your expectation of them. Make sure you explicitly tell all host teachers that this is not an observation that is in any way tied to their evaluation. Explain to them that they should be teaching from the curriculum and that you'd like to see one lesson. Make sure they understand that they do not need to prepare anything special for their guests.

Meeting with your hosts in person can help you clearly communicate your purpose and put their minds at ease that they are not being evaluated or expected to put on a show. It can also give you a better sense of their comfort level. If a teacher is feeling particularly uncomfortable at the idea of exposing his or her practice so publicly, you can adjust by giving time to coplan or support from a curriculum consultant. If possible, plan to meet with teachers at least a week or two before the lab during a common planning time, PLC, or other shared time for professional dialogue.

When communicating with principal participants hosting the lab in their buildings, make sure everyone is in the loop from the beginning. If you're a building principal planning your own lab, this won't be too hard. But if you're in the role of a consultant, coach, or central office administrator, be mindful of making sure the principals have the same clear communication as the teachers in their buildings. The last thing you want is for your host teachers to get mixed messages that could further cause anxiety.

Talking to the participants in person is always the best bet, but it's also helpful to send an email out with the key points, too. They need to understand the intention and be assured that it is about your learning and how to support them, not about evaluation. A conversation can move pretty fast, and if anyone has any questions about the details of the upcoming lab, having an email to look back on can be helpful. See Figure 8.1 for a sample email that we have used in the past.

Support for a Host Teacher

A host teacher whose classroom you're observing may come from a variety of experiences and comfort levels depending on the type of lab you're facilitating and what you're hoping to see. You may visit the classroom

FIGURE 8.1

Sample Email

Hello Teacher Leaders,

I hope that you are seeing small successes while taking on this monumental change in your classroom. I am seeing and hearing such wonderful things from teachers and students. When we last met, many of you expressed concerns about administrator evaluations during this transition to new curriculum. I am excited to report that we will be hosting a principal lab all around implementation of our new math curriculum on [date].

Administrators will be learning what teaching and learning looks like with this curriculum and will be digging into ways to support you. Attached is the document that will ground us in our instructional look-fors.

In order to enrich our experience, we are hoping to visit several classrooms in the early stages of implementation. We all know that change is messy and takes time. We are not at all expecting perfection. Our visit will not be evaluative and will not be about you. It is an experience to ground us in our own professional learning.

Thank you for considering this opportunity to help your administrative support team learn and grow. We value your leadership as we strive to provide our students the best possible learning opportunities.

Thank you,

[Name]

Adapted with permission from Waterford School District.

of a teacher leader who is typically at the forefront of the department's learning edge and is eager to be involved, or you may visit teachers who are new to curriculum or instructional practices and are feeling particularly vulnerable.

For this reason, it's imperative to prioritize the importance of building and maintaining healthy relationships with host teachers. We usually think in terms of what kinds of support hosts might need from us as facilitators before, during, and after the actual lab.

Before

In Chapter 3, we discussed our belief that principal labs are situated within a system of professional learning; so, too, should the support for your host be a part of your system. Depending on the purpose of the observation and the comfort level of the host teacher, you may connect your host to varying levels of support before the lab. All hosts will need clear communication about why you're coming, when, and what they should expect from the day, but you'll find that some appreciate more support ahead of time. To do this, turn to your system to look for opportunities. You may visit a PLC or ask a PLC to coconstruct a lesson you'll be observing, or you may have more individualized coconstruction by having the host teacher plan with a leader like a coach, consultant, or department head. Or, similarly, you may have one of those instructional leaders observe a lesson ahead of the lab and coach them about planning decisions.

Regardless of the level of coaching and support, we've found that having an informal, non-evaluative, pre-observation visit is crucial both for the host teachers and the facilitators. These help you, as facilitators, get a better idea of what to expect when you bring participants to their room, and it can give the host teacher assurances that you know what you're getting and you value them as a part of your important day of learning.

During

It's a small move but one that should not be underestimated: If you are the person who supported or recruited your host teacher, try to be the first lab participant to enter the host's room, smile, and greet them casually and quietly. Rather than making an introduction to the group, we treat this time more as a warm greeting for a coworker. This is something we've done almost innately, but we have realized in reflection that it has been an important move to build relationships and set the host at ease. Once you have several participants inside the host teacher's classroom, there's not a whole lot you can do to support them aside from having established and clearly communicated norms for how participants will interact once in the room. We'll detail this a little later in the section on logistics for participants, but if the host teacher knows ahead of time that they can expect principal lab participants to take notes on what they see and hear and observe without interacting, it helps set their minds at ease so that a somewhat high-pressure situation doesn't come with so many unknowns.

Even though a principal lab isn't about giving immediate feedback to the hosts in the experience, we know that it's natural for host teachers to wonder what participants were thinking. In the next section, we'll discuss options for more formal, structured feedback for host teachers, but we've also found that some quick, positive sticky notes with appreciative observations can be powerful tools for real-time feedback. Depending on the type of lab and the number of shared observations, you may have every lab participant leave a sticky note for the classrooms they visit, or you may have one or two facilitators leave a piece of real-time feedback. These, then, serve to support the host teachers by giving them positive reinforcement and real-time feedback in a simple way.

After

Once the shared observation is over, support for the host doesn't necessarily end. They've agreed to be an integral part in your participants' learning, so we've found that it's important to be intentional when making sure they get some structured follow-up. One way that we always do this is through thank-you notes. Once lab participants are back from shared observations and have had time to individually process and reflect on their observations, we ask each participant to fill out a blank thank-you card for the host teacher they observed. We supply the blank cards, and we've found that this can be a good use of flexible planning time. As some participants finish their reflection early, they can start their thank-you notes and give others time to finish their reflections at their own pace. Someone from the lab (a facilitator or administrator from the host's building) then agrees to deliver the completed notes to the host teacher's classroom or mailbox.

Beyond thank-you notes, there does not always need to be formal feedback to the host teacher from lab participants. Although the purpose of principal labs is to build participants' efficacy in giving feedback, this is in a broad sense, not necessarily for the isolated event of the observation itself. For this reason, you may let host teachers know that they shouldn't expect a formal follow-up with feedback from their administrators like they might in a formal or evaluative observation. However, we also recognize that some host teachers would really value more formal and critical feedback than the thank-you notes allow, so depending on the dynamics of the lab and the hosts, we have sometimes presented the host teachers with feedback options. In some cases, following the lab, host teachers may choose whether they continue their experience by reaching out through a scheduled meeting, an email, or any way that is agreeable to them.

We've also found that it's important to get feedback from our host teachers. Just as we intentionally want to hear from lab participants to shape future plans, we believe there is a lot of value in asking host teachers what the experience was like for them. You may do this by reaching out informally or through a survey. Gathering their feedback can help you better shape the norms for participants and support future lab hosts, and it can help you to grow a culture of hosting principal labs so that more teachers will continue to agree to be a part of shared observations in the future.

Logistics for Participants

If you haven't already surmised from the chapters that came before this one, our biggest piece of advice for making things run smoothly for your participants is structure, structure, structure. Planning ahead how to structure each interaction throughout the day will help you facilitate conversation that is deeply engaging, meaningful, and in which participants feel safe to be vulnerable in their learning.

Working Agreements

Garmston and Wellman (2002) of Adaptive Schools define working agreements as "agreed upon guidelines for how group members will conduct themselves to achieve meeting outcomes" (p. 44). When working with a group of administrators, it's easy to think that you can skip establishing these, but just because your participants are professionals doesn't mean you can take for granted that they all share the same language of how to work together. Administrative teams are complicated systems of their own with multi-faceted dynamics that can affect how people participate, and establishing explicit ways of interacting helps build what Amy Edmondson (2013) calls psychological safety. As Brené Brown (2018) explains,

> The behaviors that people need from their team or group almost always include listening, staying curious, being honest, and keeping confidence. Dare to lead by investing twenty minutes in creating psychological safety when you need to rumble [with vulnerability]. Make your intention of

creating safety explicit and get your team's help on how to do it effectively. (p. 37)

To that end, we believe that these are most effective when they're coconstructed, so we like to ask participants to contribute descriptors of what effective participation and learning look like to them. To ensure that these stay rooted in a culture of vulnerability and valued voices, it's important that you facilitate a discussion that guides participants to look for the markers of effective collaboration when

- Everyone's voice is heard.
- Participation is equally distributed.
- Active participation is needed.
- Everyone is open to new learning, opinions, and ideas.
- Learning happens within a space that is safe for all participants.
- Learning within the lab influences life outside it.

Observation Norms

Just as you have working agreements for the participants' learning, it's important to outline what to expect and how to interact within shared observations. Because participants are not taking on so much vulnerability in this role, we have not prioritized the coconstruction of these norms like we have with working agreements. Instead, we typically remind participants of the established norms before each observation. The overall purpose of the norms is more important than how you might word each one. Having clear expectations lets participants know how to interact in a way that is least distracting to the teachers and students in the room and will give them the most authentic observation possible. In working with different groups around observation norms, we've heard some borrow from scouting norms to say, "Leave no trace," and others have put it more playfully: "Enter and leave like a ninja." You may also share norms about where participants should position themselves around the room. Some host teachers may have additional desks available, and others may ask that you stand around the perimeter of the room. We've found that it's sometimes helpful to let participants know that they are encouraged to circulate through the room when students are working independently or collaboratively so that they can better see and hear what students are working on. However you word your norms, ensure all participants know to resist inserting themselves into lessons and instead focus on observing the lesson as it unfolds naturally.

Discussion Protocols

Similar to building and checking back in on norms, structuring opportunities for discussion with specific protocols isn't something that is always the first thing you think about when planning for principals as your audience. But, even though they may be highly adept at discussion skills, tightly structured protocols help ensure that everyone is equitably invited to participate. In an article examining the power of protocols in equitable instruction for students, Hammond (2020) explains, "The overly structured nature of protocols might seem counterintuitive to the goal of encouraging a free-flowing discussion that welcomes all students. In reality, it is just the opposite. Protocols create ways into the discussion for students typically left out." So, too, do protocols create ways into the discussion for adult learners. Depending on the dynamics of your leaders and the learning they're embarking on, you may engage participants in a variety of protocols to bring out the most productive discussions. Throughout Chapters 4–7 of this book, we share some discussion protocol examples that we've used to intentionally structure conversation in each type of lab, but ultimately, what's most important is choosing protocols that ensure everyone is equitably able to participate in thinking and discussing the day's learning—no matter the lab type.

Surveys and Feedback

When we first established principal labs as a regular part of our professional learning calendar, we were careful about thoughtfully including participants' voices. We heard from administrators from each building separately during our regularly scheduled school improvement meetings, but we also wanted to explicitly discuss how these labs could be of service to them. So, early in our first lab of the school year, we structured a discussion where we asked participants what they'd like to get out of these regular opportunities for their own learning, and we charted their answers. At the end of the lab and again at subsequent labs, we checked back in to see how we were doing, how we might pivot, and what we might need to add. As the labs progressed, we continued to get this kind of input through exit tickets and electronic surveys before and after the labs themselves. Doing this helped us as facilitators plan for learning that was relevant, and it helped participants know that their input was valued.

Celebrate Success

Participants aren't going to open up and be vulnerable with their colleagues if they feel as though they are always the ones in need, so it's important to celebrate what's going well. Brown (2018) frames this example of daring leadership as "practicing gratitude and celebrating milestones and victories," and it directly contradicts her example of "armored leadership" in which ineffective leaders are "working from scarcity and squandering opportunities for joy and recognition" (p. 77). If participants can feel like problem solvers at the table, they're also more likely to be vulnerable with their own problems of practice, and, as facilitators, you can build learning on the foundations of appreciative inquiry.

Whether through the points of pride celebrations at the beginning of a lab or by grouping participants together with their successes and strengths in mind, we believe it's important to intentionally plan for opportunities to have participants share celebrations, successes, and problems that they're successfully solving. This helps us establish a cultural frame built upon the premise that "organizations and the people in them do not need to be fixed, but instead affirmed, so that they can build on the resources and skills they already have" (Henderson et al., 2011, p. 3).

As you begin planning for principal labs, it's easy to get bogged down in the logistics, but if you keep celebrating successes and affirming the hard work that you're all doing at the center of your planning, you'll establish a culture where instructional leaders form partnerships to lead and learn together.

Conclusion: The Heart of Principal Labs

In all labs, you will make adjustments and readjustments. If you anchor your planning in the four elements—relationship building, an anchoring experience, shared observation, and feedback and feeding forward—you'll use a flowchart like the one in Figure 8.2 to help you make decisions to build your day's agenda. Ultimately, you may end up planning labs that mirror our sample agendas almost exactly, and you'll likely run some that vary to meet the unique needs of your group. You may develop new types of principal labs to study the learning edge that you need in that moment. But above all else the heart of your labs will always stay grounded in these foundational components:

- **Share the vision.** Gain a stronger understanding of effective practices by grounding your conversations in a shared experience so that administrators can support learning with greater comfort, context level, and confidence.
- **Calibrate and celebrate.** Develop an understanding of where students, teachers, and buildings are on the continuum of implementation, and celebrate their transition to the vision.
- **Mentor through the messiness.** Lift the voices and experiences of teachers and principals to understand their needs. Practice how to give feedback that will support risktaking as everyone works toward a common vision.

With principals filling the shoes of some of the most influential roles in a school and with their responsibilities as instructional leaders increasing, professional learning for principals has never been more important. We initially invested our time in principal labs because we recognized the need for specially designed opportunities to learn in a setting that allows principals to embrace their vulnerability with each other. Now, more than five years since we facilitated our first principal lab, we recognize its tremendous impact more than ever. We believe that incorporating this professional learning structure was one of the most effective moves we have made when working to build a supportive system focused on teacher, leader, and student growth. Principal labs offered us the opportunity to move the principalship from an isolated endeavor to a network of instructional leaders. And that is our greatest hope in sharing principal labs with you: that you may build principal labs that help you strengthen instructional leadership through shared learning.

FIGURE 8.2

Structure Flowchart

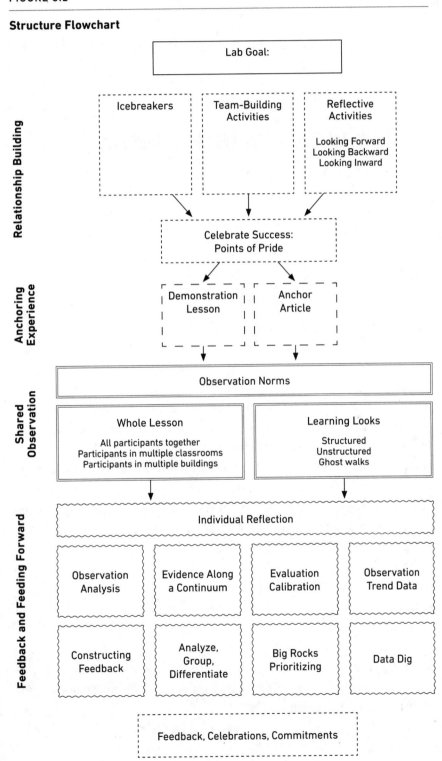

Acknowledgments

First and foremost, thank you to the original "dream team." The real magic in our work was in collaboration, and we are so thankful for all of you. We want to especially recognize Joe, Chris, Lauren, and Shannon for planning and facilitating countless learning labs together and for dreaming together with us about how to better support and collaborate with instructional leaders. Sharing with you the commitment to learn, to reflect on our facilitation, and to plan for impactful professional learning is what shaped principal labs. We count ourselves lucky to get to write about this incredible work. Joe, we are additionally thankful for the conversation and reflection you prompted when we first started writing about this project. Lisa, thank you for your guidance, for reading through some of our early thinking, and most of all, for believing in us and in the power of principals learning together.

Thank you to the principals who were part of our first labs and to those who we've continued to work with since. We are thankful to know so many lead learners, and we have been so fortunate to learn together in community with you.

To the teachers who have been part of our principal labs, we are endlessly inspired by your leadership, your vulnerability, and your willingness to share your practice so that others may learn. Thank you for inviting us into your classrooms.

To the Job-Embedded Professional Learning Network, we are grateful to be surrounded by such an incredible group of instructional leaders who consistently challenge us to grow. Thank you for coming together to support each other in learning and leadership.

We also want to thank our editing team at ASCD. To Susan Hills, thank you for recognizing that there was a book in our idea and helping us shape it into existence. Your questions helped us reflect and keep learning throughout our writing. Thank you to Megan Doyle and the graphic team for making our work sparkle on the page.

Finally, thank you to our families. Scott, Joe, Alex, Jack, Charlotte, Owen, Jacob, Jake, and Jolie, you have given us up for so many weekends and evenings, and you've been our biggest cheerleaders. You keep us going. We love you.

Appendix: The Clipboard

We call this appendix the "clipboard." Whenever we facilitate a principal lab, a clipboard is one of our most essential tools. You may use our clipboard materials and ideas to get you started, and you can even download any of these forms from www.ascd.org/theclipboard. However, we hope that you'll adapt these resources to make principal labs a structure for professional learning that will fit the unique and changing needs of the principals you work with.

FIGURE A.1

Structure Flowchart

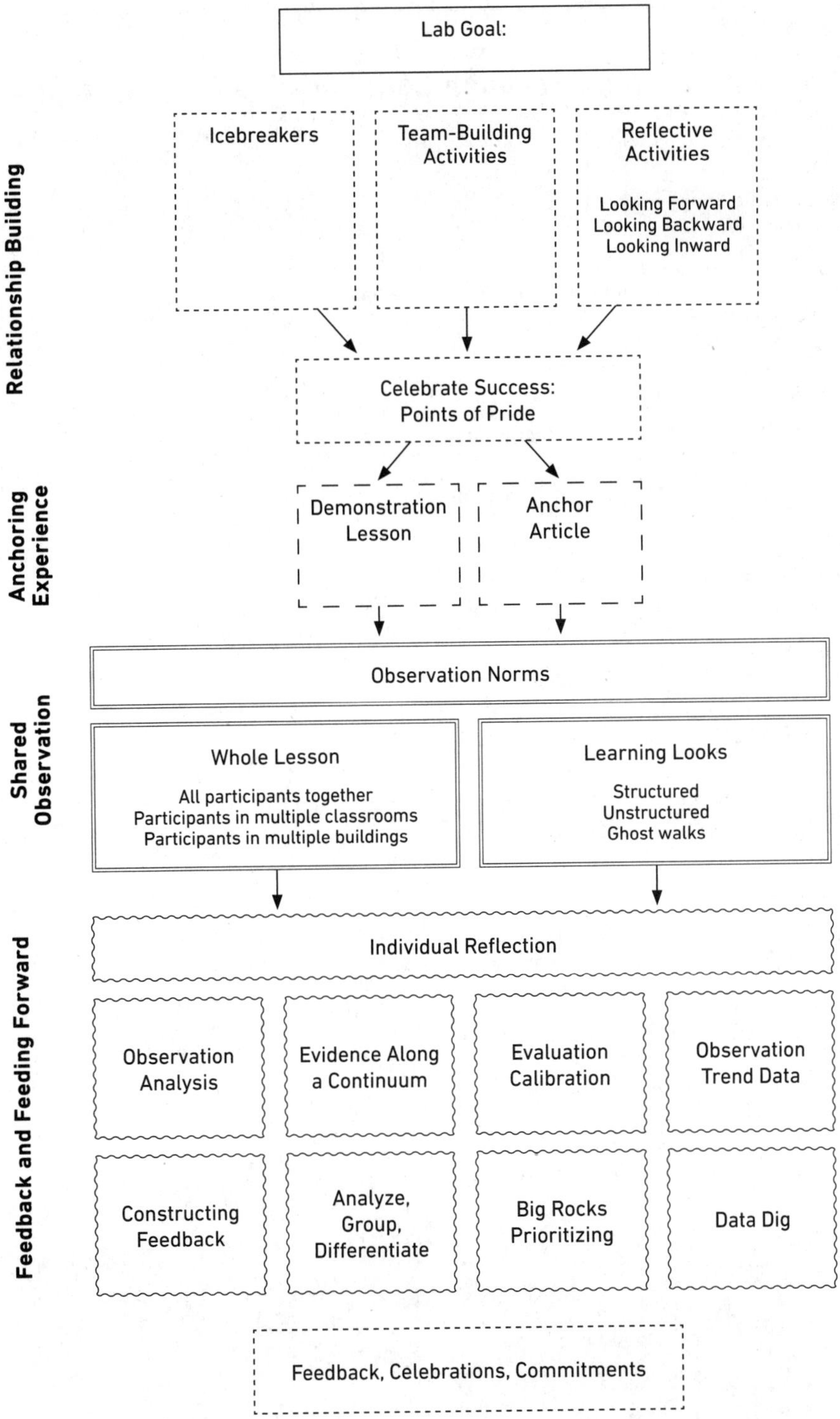

Relationship Building

Lab Goal:

Icebreakers

Team-Building
Activities

Reflective
Activities

Looking Forward
Looking Backward
Looking Inward

Celebrate Success:
Points of Pride

Anchoring Experience

Demonstration
Lesson

Anchor
Article

Shared Observation

Observation Norms

Whole Lesson

All participants together
Participants in multiple classrooms
Participants in multiple buildings

Learning Looks

Structured
Unstructured
Ghost walks

Feedback and Feeding Forward

Individual Reflection

Observation
Analysis

Evidence Along
a Continuum

Evaluation
Calibration

Observation
Trend Data

Constructing
Feedback

Analyze,
Group,
Differentiate

Big Rocks
Prioritizing

Data Dig

Feedback, Celebrations, Commitments

FIGURE A.2

Principal Lab Agenda

Leading and Learning Through Collaborative Partnerships

Morning

Relationship Building
- Connector
- Points of Pride

Anchoring Experience: Model Lesson or Shared Reading
Shared Observation
Feedback and Feeding Forward
- Individual Reflection
- Observation Analysis

Lunch and Thank-You Notes to Teacher Hosts

Afternoon

Data Dig
Responsive Planning
Reflection
- How will today's experience influence your work in your building tomorrow?

Thinking Ahead
- What additional support could we provide?
- How can we design the next principal lab experience to best meet your learning needs?

Adapted with permission from Waterford School District.

FIGURE A.3

GIVE Reflection

G	I	V	E
Something I *grasp* in my new learning.	*I'm* feeling nervous about . . .	The next *viable* step for me in enacting this learning is . . .	Please *extend* support that looks like _____ to help me be successful in this.

FIGURE A.4

Curriculum Observation Template

Structure	Noticings (see/hear)	Connection to GIVE
Beginning		
Middle		
End		

FIGURE A.5

Instructional Continuum Guide

Initial Indicators	Partial Implementation	Full Implementation
What will you see or hear that supports first steps in implementation?	What will you see or hear to show ongoing attempts at implementation?	When will you know that the indicator has become a part of daily practice?

Staffwide and individual teacher celebrations:

Full implementation of this component over time will result in:

FIGURE A.6

Instruction Observation Template

	Noticings (see/hear)	Connection to ICG
Teacher		
Student		

FIGURE A.7

Learning Looks Observation Template

	Student Behaviors (see/hear)	Teacher Behaviors (see/hear)
Room # _____		
Room # _____		
Room # _____		

FIGURE A.8

Aspirations Observation Template

Focus: _____

Questions/Wonders	Notes
Shifts in My Thinking	Takeaways/Next Steps

FIGURE A.9

Learning Looks Organizer: Inferences and Feedback

Grade Level: _____

What do you see/hear? (the observed facts)	Why might that be? (the present context)	What might you say? (feedback for growth)

References

Aguilar, E. (2018). *Onward: Cultivating emotional resilience in educators*. San Francisco: Jossey-Bass.

Brown. B. (2018). *Dare to lead: Brave work, tough conversations, whole hearts*. New York: Random House.

CASEL. (2020). SEL: What are the core competencies and where are they promoted? Retrieved from https://casel.org/core-competencies/

Cooperrider, D. L., & Whitney, D. K. (2005). *Appreciative inquiry: A positive revolution in change*. San Francisco: Berrett-Koehler.

Covey, S. R. (2018). Big rocks: Stephen R. Covey. [Video]. Retrieved from https://resources.franklincovey.com/the-8th-habit/big-rocks-stephen-r-covey

Covey, S. R., Merrill, R. A., & Merrill, R. R. (1995). *First things first*. New York: Simon & Schuster.

Danielson, C. (2007). *Enhancing professional practice: A framework for teaching* (2nd ed.). Alexandria, VA: ASCD.

Darling-Hammond, L., Hyler, M. E., & Gardner, M. (2017). *Effective teacher professional development*. Palo Alto, CA: Learning Policy Institute.

Dobbs, C. L., Ippolito, J., & Charner-Laird, M. (2017). *Investigating disciplinary literacy: A framework for collaborative professional learning*. Cambridge, MA: Harvard Education Press.

Donohoo, J. (2013). *Collaborative inquiry for educators: A facilitator's guide to school improvement*. Thousand Oaks, CA: Corwin.

Edmondson, A. C. (2013). *Teaming: How organizations learn, innovate, and compete in the knowledge economy*. San Francisco: Jossey-Bass.

Fullan, M. (2002, May). The change leader. *Educational Leadership, 59*(8), 16–21.

Fullan, M., & Sharratt, L. (2007). Sustaining leadership in complex times. In B. Davies (Ed.), *Developing sustainable leadership*. London: Paul Chapman.

Fullan, M., & Quinn, J. (2016). *Coherence: The right drivers in action for schools, districts, and systems*. Thousand Oaks, CA: Corwin.

Gallagher, A., & Thordarson, K. (2018). *Design thinking for school leaders: Five roles and mindsets that ignite positive change*. Alexandria, VA: ASCD.

Garcia, E., & Weiss, E. (2019). *The teacher shortage is real, large and growing, and worse than we thought*. Washington, D.C.: Economic Policy Institute.

Garmston, R. J., & Wellman, B. M. (2002). *The adaptive school: Developing and facilitating collaborative groups.* Norwood, MA: Christopher-Gordon.

Gruenert, S., & Whitaker, T. (2015). *School culture rewired: How to define, assess, and transform it.* Alexandria, VA: ASCD.

Hammond, Z. (2020, April). The power of protocols for equity. *Educational Leadership, 77*(7), 45–50.

Hammond, Z., & Jackson, Y. (2015). *Culturally responsive teaching and the brain: Promoting authentic engagement and rigor among culturally and linguistically diverse students.* Thousand Oaks, CA: Corwin.

Harhsak, A., Aguirre, D., & Brown, A. (2010). *Making change happen, and making it stick: Delivering sustainable organizational change.* New York: Booz.

Hattie, J. (2015). High-impact leadership. *Educational Leadership, 72*(5), 36–40.

Hattie, J., Fisher, D., Frey, N., Gojak, L. M., Moore, S. D., & Mellman, W. (2017). *Visible learning for mathematics: What works best to optimize student learning, grades K–12.* Thousand Oaks, CA: Corwin.

Heifetz, R., & Linsky, M. (2002, June). A survival guide for leaders. *Harvard Business Review.* Retrieved from https://hbr.org/2002/06/a-survival-guide-for-leaders

Henderson, M., Lee, S., Whitaker, G., & Altman, L. (2011) Positive problem solving: How appreciative inquiry works. *ICMA Press, 43*(3).

Joyce, B., & Showers, B. (2002). *Student achievement through staff development* (3rd ed.). Alexandria, VA: ASCD.

Kaplinsky, R. (2016, August 15). #Observe me. Retrieved from https://robertkaplinsky.com/observeme/

Killion, J. (2013). *Comprehensive professional learning system: A workbook for states and districts.* Oxford, OH: Learning Forward.

Learning Forward. (2021, January 11). Learning communities. Retrieved from https://learningforward.org/standards/learning-communities/

Loewus, L. (2018, December 6). Millennial teachers: Things to consider in trying to recruit and retain them. *EdWeek.* Retrieved from https://blogs.edweek.org/teachers/teaching_now/2018/12/millennial_teachers_things_to_consider_in_trying_to_recruit_and_retain_them.html

Many, T. W., Maffoni, M. J., Sparks, S. K., & Thomas, T. F. (2018). *Amplify your impact: Coaching collaborative teams in PLCs.* Bloomington, IN: Solution Tree.

Martin, J. (2019, February). Turning around schools: The real key to success. *Principal Leadership, 19.* Retrieved from https://www.nassp.org/publication/principal-leadership/volume-19-2018-2019/principal-leadership-february-2019/turning-around-schools-the-real-key-to-success/

NASSP & NAESP. (2013). *Leadership matters: What the research says about the importance of principal leadership.* Reston, VA & Alexandria, VA: Authors.

Newkirk, T. (2017). *Embarrassment: And the emotional underlife of learning.* Portsmouth, NH: Heinemann.

Reeves, D. B. (2009). *Leading change in your school: How to conquer myths, build commitment, and get results.* Alexandria, VA: ASCD

Robinson, V. (2011). *Student-centered leadership.* San Francisco: Jossey-Bass.

Sawyer, I., & Stukey, M. R. (2019). *Professional learning redefined: An evidence-based guide.* Thousand Oaks: Corwin.

School Reform Initiative. (2017a, March 30). Four A's text protocol. Retrieved from https://www.schoolreforminitiative.org/download/four-as-text-protocol/

School Reform Initiative. (2017b, March 30). Ghost visit. Retrieved from https://www.schoolreforminitiative.org/download/ghost-visit/

Spillane, J., Halverson, R., & Diamond, D. (2001). Investigating school leadership practice: A distributive perspective. *Educational Researcher, 30*(3).

Stein, M. K., & Nelson, B. S. (2003, December). Leadership content knowledge. *Educational Evaluation and Policy Analysis, 25*(4), 423–448.

Strong, R., Silver, H., & Robinson, A. (1995). Strengthening student engagement: What do students really want (and what really motivates them)? *Educational Leadership, 53*(1), 8–12.

Tomlinson, C. A. (2017). *How to differentiate instruction in academically diverse classrooms* (3rd ed.). Alexandria, VA: ASCD.

Index

The letter *f* following a page number denotes a figure.

agendas, sample
- Aspirations, 104*f*
- Growing the Network, 86*f*
- Instructional Best Practice, 64*f*
- Leading and Learning Through Collaborative Partnerships, 25*f*, 138*f*
- Math Curriculum Adoption, 44*f*

anchor articles, 14–15, 108–109

anchoring experience
- anchor articles, 14–15, 108–109
- components suggested in, 11*f*
- demonstration lessons, 14–15
- fostering collaborative aspirations labs, 108–109
- instructional practices labs, 76–77
- network of leaders labs, 94–96
- new curriculum introduction labs, 52–55
- shared learning in the, 14

appreciative inquiry (AI) approach, 99

aspirations, fostering collaborative
- anchoring experience, 108–109
- determining focus, 109–111
- feedback and feeding forward, 112–116
- focus, target, shared observations, 26*f*
- introduction, 105–106
- relationship building, 106–108
- sample agenda, 104*f*
- shared observation, 111–112, 113*f*

aspirations, fostering collaborative, planning for
- approach to observations, 111–112
- celebrations, 106–107
- deepening understanding of collaborative teamwork, 107–108
- participants determining a meaningful focus, 109–111
- protocols to structure discussion, 112–116
- shared experience with different areas of focus, 108–109
- where to observe, 111

Aspirations Observation Template, 144*f*

awkwardness principle, 46, 55

back-to-back drawings activity, 92–93

balcony-level perspective, 96

big rocks prioritizing, 60–61

book study, 115–116

celebrations, 13–14, 100–101, 106–107, 130–132

circles, using in labs, 122

coaches, for principals, 2

coaching
- collaborative, 21, 22

coaching (*continued*)
 for participant ownership, 21
collaboration. *See also* aspirations, fostering collaborative
 fostering over competition, 36–37
 #WSDcollaborates, 81
 for principals, importance of, 87, 88–89
collaborative culture, building a, 1–2
Collaborative Learning ICG, 71*f*
competitive culture, moving away from, 36–37
connectors
 instructional practices labs, 74–75
 new curriculum introduction labs, 50–51
 relationship building, 92, 107–108
curiosity, generating for implementation, 37–39
Curriculum Observation Template, 58*f*, 140*f*

data, for feedback and feeding forward, 20–21, 84–85
demonstration lessons, 14–15
discussion, structuring
 to build relationships, 13
 to foster collaborative observation, 115
 to identify the next steps forward, 99–101
 observations to prepare for, 98–99
 protocols, 112–116
discussion and debriefing, structuring
 to analyze and group observation data to differentiate support, 84–85
 big rocks prioritizing, 60–61
 to cocreate success indicators, 83
 cross-pollination through varied grouping, 59
 evaluation calibration, 60
 observation groups to construct feedback, 61–62
 observations evidence on a continuum, 83–84
 to prioritize feedback, 59–60
dyad and triad debriefing, 113–114

evaluations, disconnecting observations from, 39–41
evaluators, awkwardness principle and, 46–47

experience, anchoring. *See* anchoring experience
feedback
 awkwardness principle and, 46–47
 back-to-back drawings activity, 93
 #observeme, 80
 observation conversations, asset-based, 100–101
 priming participants for, 55
feedback and feeding forward
 beginning the work of, 22
 collaborative coaching in, 21, 22
 components suggested in, 11*f*
 data for, 20–21, 84–85
 fostering collaborative aspirations labs, 112–116
 importance of, 19, 35
 instructional practices labs, 83–85
 making a commitment to, 21–22
 network of leaders labs, 99–103
 new curriculum introduction labs, 59–62
 observation analysis in, 20, 35–36
 planning intentionally for teachers' needs, 22–23
 reflection element, 20, 21–22
 shifting to a culture of vs. evaluation, 40–41
 structuring, 19–20

ghost visits, 18–19
GIVE reflection protocol, 53–54, 54*f*, 59, 60, 139*f*
grit mentality, 53
groups
 cross-pollinate through variation in, 59
 large, offer two dates for the same lab, 119
 network of leaders labs, 94–95
 new curriculum introduction labs, 51–52
 in relationship building, 12–13
 shared observation, 17
 structuring discussion and debriefing in, 59–62

host classrooms, choosing, 16–17, 77–79, 111
host teachers, logistics for
 choosing and preparing, 55–57
 communications, 40, 123–124, 125*f*
 feedback to and from, 127–128
 supports, 124–128

host teachers, logistics for (*continued*)
thank-you notes to, 130–131

icebreakers, 12
"If, Then" frame, 112
implementation, beliefs at the core of
successful
all participants are valuable, 32–33
all voices need to be heard, 32–33
authors' experiences in, 27–28
learning is valuable, 31
power in collaborative inquiry and
its vulnerability, 32
shared vision is fundamental,
28–29, 132
they exist within a system for professional learning, 29–31
implementation, beliefs into practice
authors' experiences in, 33–34
by busting competition and building collaboration, 36–37
by disconnecting evaluations and
observations, 39
by embracing being an instructional leader, 34–36
by generating interest and curiosity, 37–39
implementation, elements essential to,
11*f*
inquiry, power in collaborative, 32
Instructional Continuum Guide (ICG),
69–70, 71*f*, 72–73, 141*f*
instructional leader. *See also* network of
leaders labs
embracing being an, 34–36
taking time to become an, 34–36
instructional practices
compartmentalizing in, 68
requirements for changing, 9
instructional practices labs
anchoring experience, 76–77
determining focus, 66–73
feedback and feeding forward,
83–85
focus, target, shared observations,
26*f*
introduction, 65–66
relationship building, 73–75
sample agenda, 64*f*
shared observation, 77–83, 78*f*, 81*f*,
82*f*
instructional practices labs, planning for
connectors, 74–75

instructional practices labs, planning for
(*continued*)
creating a shared understanding of
the instruction, 76–77
identifying practices that will get
to what you value in instruction,
67–68
identifying success indicators,
69–70, 71*f*, 72–73
identifying your values in instruction, 66–67
inviting participants to engage with
the observation, 81, 83
participants, 73–74
structuring discussion and debriefing, 83–85
structuring the lab space, 76
success indicators, cocreating, 83
which classrooms to visit, 77–81,
78*f*, 81*f*, 82*f*
Instruction Observation Template, 78*f*,
142*f*

lab space, structuring the
circles as the basis of, 122
instructional practices labs, planning for, 76
introduction, 122
to keep learning visible, 123
seating arrangements, 122
leaders. *See* instructional leaders; network of leaders labs
lead learner, becoming a, 2
learning
keeping visible in the lab space, 123
value of, 31
learning community, requirements of a, 3
learning looks, structured and unstructured, 17–18, 79–80
Learning Looks Observation Template,
81*f*, 143*f*
Learning Looks Organizer: Inferences
and Feedback, 145*f*
logistics, for participants
celebrate success, 130–131
discussion protocols, 130
feedback and surveys, 130–131
observation norms, 129–130
working agreements, 128–129
logistics, for the host teacher
communications, 123–124, 125*f*
feedback to and from, 127–128
supports, 124–128
thank-you notes to, 130–131

logistics, scheduling
    categorizing interruptions, 42
    emergencies, recognizing, 42
    introduction, 117–118
    location, 121–122
    logistics, 41–42
    managing the messiness, 42
    participants recommended,
      120–121
    series implementation, 118
logistics, structuring the lab space
    circles as the basis of, 122
    instructional practices labs, plan-
      ning for, 76
    introduction, 122
    keep learning visible, 123
    planning for instructional practices
      labs, 76
    seating arrangements, 122

messiness
    managing the, 42
    mentoring through, 132
millennials in the workforce, 2–3

network of leaders labs
    anchoring experience, 94–96
    connector activity, 92
    determining focus, 88–92
    feedback and feeding forward,
      99–103
    focus, target, shared observations,
      26*f*
    introduction, 87–88
    observation conversations, asset-
      based, 100–101
    relationship building, 92–94
    sample agenda, 86*f*
    shared observation, 96–99
network of leaders labs, planning for
    building perspective through
      observation, 96–97
    engaging participants in shared
      learning, 94–96
    groupings, 94–95
    how to build leadership, 92
    identifying areas needing support,
      89–90
    identifying the need for growing
      the network, 88–89
    laying the groundwork for team-
      work, 92–94
    ongoing supports, 101–103

network of leaders labs, planning for
    (*continued*)
    organizing observation notes, 97,
      98*f*
    participants, recruiting, 90–92, 91*f*
    structuring discussions to identify
      next steps forward within a safe
      culture for learning, 99–101
    structuring observation to prepare
      participants for discussions,
      98–99
new curriculum introduction labs
    anchoring experience, 52–55
    determining focus, 46–50
    feedback and feeding forward,
      59–62
    focus, target, shared observations,
      26*f*
    introduction, 45–46
    participants, priming for feedback,
      55
    participants recommended,
      120–121
    relationship building, 50–52
    sample agenda, 44*f*, 64*f*
    shared observation, 55–57, 58*f*
new curriculum introduction labs, planning for
    approaching the focus of support,
      46–47
    choosing and preparing host teach-
      ers, 55–57
    groupings, 51–52
    identifying content area(s) imple-
      menting curriculum or stan-
      dards, 47–48
    identifying what in the new curric-
      ulum is different, 48–49
    instructional supports, 48–49
    making connectors meaningful,
      50–51
    structuring discussion and debrief-
      ing, 59–61
    structuring observations, 57, 58*f*
    what you want the team to under-
      stand, 52–54
Now and Later taffy candy questions,
  21–22

observation analysis
    analyze and group data to, differen-
      tiate support, 84–85
    evidence on a continuum, 83–84

observation analysis (*continued*)
  in feedback and feeding forward,
    20, 35–36
  groups to construct feedback,
    61–62
  network of leaders labs, 100–101
  observation sort, 100
  paired perspectives, 100
observations. *See also* shared observation
  collaborative planning following,
    101
  conversations, network of leaders
    labs, 100–101
  disconnecting evaluations from,
    39–41
  participants, logistics for, 129–130
observations, planning for
  an approach to, 111–112
  building perspective through,
    96–97
  inviting participants to engage, 81,
    83
  organizing notes, 97, 98*f*
  structuring of, 57, 58*f*
  structuring to prepare for discus-
    sions, 98–99
  where to observe, 111

participants
  instructional practices labs, plan-
    ning for, 73–74
  recruiting for network of leaders
    labs, 90–92, 91*f*
  responsive planning for, 23, 24–25*f*,
    25–26
  shared learning, planning for,
    94–96
participants, logistics for
  celebrate success, 130–131
  discussion protocols, 130
  feedback and surveys, 130–131
  observation norms, 129–130
  working agreements, 128–129
participants, recommended
  instructional practices labs, 73–74
  new curriculum labs, 120–121
  principal labs, 9–10, 36
  scheduling logistics, 120–121
points of pride, celebrating, 13–14,
  106–107
postholing, 45–46
principal labs. *See also specific elements*
  emotional work of, 11, 16
  foundational components, 132

principal labs. *See also specific elements*
  (*continued*)
  impacts of, 5–6
  introduction to, 5
  participants recommended, 9–10,
    36
  types of, 26*f*
principal labs, planning for. *See also*
  logistics
  breaks, 119–120
  grace time, 119
  laying the groundwork as you go, 43
  lunch, 120
  modeling the importance of learn-
    ing, 120
  substitutes, 119
  visioning the lab itself, 43
principal labs, planning tools
  Aspirations Observation Template,
    144*f*
  The Clipboard, 136–145
  Curriculum Observation Template,
    140*f*
  GIVE reflection protocol, 139*f*
  Instructional Continuum Guide
    (ICG), 141*f*
  Instruction Observation Template,
    142*f*
  Learning Looks Observation Tem-
    plate, 143*f*
  Learning Looks Organizer: Infer-
    ences and Feedback, 145*f*
  sample agendas, 25*f*, 44*f*, 64*f*, 86*f*,
    104*f*, 138*f*
  structure flowchart, 24*f*, 137*f*
principals
  coaches for, 2
  generating interest and curiosity
    among, 37–38
  as lead learners, 2
  professional learning for, 1–4
  teams, need for, 88–89
professional learning
  goals for, 4–5
  introduction, 1–4
  principal labs within a system for,
    5, 29–31
  standards, 3
  value in, 31, 41, 118–119

reflection, 12, 20, 21–22
relationship building
  activities for, 12, 92, 107–108
  among stakeholders, 10–12

relationship building (*continued*)
    components suggested in, 11*f*
    discussions, structuring, 13
    fostering collaborative aspirations
      labs, 106–108
    groupings, 12–13
    instructional practices labs, 73–75
    network of leaders labs, 92–94
    new curriculum introduction labs,
      50–52
    points of pride, celebrating, 13–14,
      106–107
risk-taking, vulnerability in, 53–55, 54*f*

seating arrangements in labs, 122
shared observation. *See also* host classrooms, choosing; observations
    balcony-level perspective, 96
    components suggested in, 11*f*
    fostering collaborative aspirations
      labs, 111–112, 113*f*
    ghost visits, 18–19
    groupings, 17
    instructional practices labs, 77–83,
      78*f*, 81*f*, 82*f*
    Instruction Observation Template,
      78*f*, 142*f*
    learning looks, structured and
      unstructured, 17–18, 79–80
    Learning Looks Observation Tem-
      plate, 81*f*, 143*f*
    Learning Looks Structured Sched-
      ule, 82*f*
    network of leaders labs, 96–99
    new curriculum introduction labs,
      55–57, 58*f*
    whole lesson, 17
silos, 68
staff development, effective, 21
Strategy Implementation Guide (SIG),
  69

taffy candy Now and Later questions,
  21–22
teachers
    credentialed, shortage of, 2–3
    evaluations, disconnecting observa-
      tion from, 39–41
    generating interest and curiosity
      among, 38–39
    host classrooms for observing,
      16–17, 40–41, 77–79, 111
    understanding principal labs,
      importance of, 40–41
team-building activities, 12
teams, principals need for, 88–89
teamwork. *See also* relationship building
    back-to-back drawings activity, 92
    collaborative, understanding,
      107–108
    laying the groundwork for, 92–94
thank-you notes, 130–131

value
    of all participants, 32–33
    of learning, 31
    in professional learning, 31, 41,
      118–119
visioning work, 28–29, 43, 132
vulnerability
    admitting, supporting, 49–50
    in curriculum implementation,
      46–47
    power in, 32
    in risk-taking, 53–55, 54*f*
    shame and, 49

whole-group calibration to prioritize
  feedback, 59–60
whole lesson shared observation, 17

About the Authors

 **Megan Kortlandt** is a literacy consultant with Oakland Schools, an intermediate school district that serves across one of Michigan's largest counties. She has taught in middle and high school classrooms in a variety of settings over the past 15 years, but she has more recently found a passion for supporting teachers and leaders as they strive to reach all learners through engagement, authenticity, and autonomy. When she's not teaching or facilitating professional learning, chances are good Megan is writing about it. She has previously been published in NCTE's journal *Voices from the Middle* and *The Michigan Reading Journal,* and she is a contributing writer for *Moving Writers*. You can find her on Twitter @megankortlandt.

 **Carly Stone** is the executive director of curriculum and instruction for the Brandon School District in Michigan. With 16 years of experience in education, she has previously worked as a math and science teacher, a building administrator for both middle and high schools, and as a K–12 director of curriculum, instruction, and assessment for one of the largest public school districts in Michigan. Over the past seven years, she has served

on multiple AdvancED/Cognia accreditation review teams studying and supporting schools and systems. She led the curriculum, instruction, and assessment department for the Waterford School District for six years as it developed not only curriculum but also professional learning around instructional practices for K–12 teachers and administrators. She finds tremendous enjoyment working directly with building principals through coaching and designing professional learning intentionally designed to meet leaders' professional goals for themselves, the schools in which they work, the teachers they support, and the students that they serve. You can find her on Twitter @CarlyStone_PL.

Samantha Keesling, EdS, is a mathematics consultant in the leadership and school improvement unit at Oakland Schools Intermediate School District. In addition to 13 years working with students and teachers in the classroom, she served on the executive board of the Detroit Area Council of Teachers of Mathematics and is a past president. For the past nine years, she has led teachers and administrators in implementing student-centered math instruction. In her role at Oakland Schools, Samantha works with Megan to coordinate the Job-Embedded Professional Learning Network, which supports instructional leaders across the region in studying, designing, and facilitating professional learning. You can find her on Twitter @Keesling_Math.

Related ASCD Resources: Professional Development

At the time of publication, the following resources were available (ASCD stock numbers in parentheses).

Print Products

The Coach Approach to School Leadership: Leading Teachers to Higher Levels of Effectiveness by Jessica Johnson, Shira Leibowitz, and Kathy Perret (#117025)

Compassionate Coaching: How to Help Educators Navigate Barriers to Professional Growth by Kathy Perret and Kenny McKee (#121017)

The eCoaching Continuum for Educators: Using Technology to Enrich Professional Development and Improve Student Outcomes by Marcia Rock (#117048)

Leading In Sync: Teacher Leaders and Principals Working Together for Student Learning by Jill Harrison Berg (#118021)

The Learning Leader: How to Focus School Improvement for Better Results, 2nd Edition by Douglas B. Reeves (#118003)

The PD Curator: How to Design Peer-to-Peer Professional Learning That Elevates Teachers and Teaching by Lauren Porosoff (#121029)

The Principal Influence: A Framework for Developing Leadership Capacity in Principals by Pete Hall, Deborah Childs-Bowen, Ann Cunningham-Morris, Phyllis Pajardo, and Alisa Simeral (#116026)

Qualities of Effective Principals, 2nd Edition by James H. Stronge and Xianxuan Xu (#121022)

Unstuck: How Curiosity, Peer Coaching, and Teaming Can Change Your School by Bryan Goodwin, Tonia Gibson, Dale Lewis, and Kris Rouleau (#118036)

For up-to-date information about ASCD resources, go to **www.ascd.org**. You can search the complete archives of Educational Leadership at **www.ascd.org/el.**

ASCD myTeachSource®

Download resources from a professional learning platform with hundreds of research-based best practices and tools for your classroom at http://myteachsource.ascd.org

For more information, send an email to member@ascd.org; call 1-800-933-2723 or 703-578-9600; send a fax to 703-575-5400; or write to Information Services, ASCD, 1703 N. Beauregard St., Alexandria, VA 22311-1714 USA.

WHOLE CHILD
TENETS

1 **HEALTHY**
Each student enters school healthy and learns about and practices a healthy lifestyle.

2 **SAFE**
Each student learns in an environment that is physically and emotionally safe for students and adults.

3 **ENGAGED**
Each student is actively engaged in learning and is connected to the school and broader community.

4 **SUPPORTED**
Each student has access to personalized learning and is supported by qualified, caring adults.

5 **CHALLENGED**
Each student is challenged academically and prepared for success in college or further study and for employment and participation in a global environment.

The ASCD Whole Child approach is an effort to transition from a focus on narrowly defined academic achievement to one that promotes the long-term development and success of all children. Through this approach, ASCD supports educators, families, community members, and policymakers as they move from a vision about educating the whole child to sustainable, collaborative actions.

Principal Labs relates to the **healthy**, **safe**, **engaged**, **supported**, and **challenged** tenets.

For more about the ASCD Whole Child approach, visit
www.ascd.org/wholechild.